Returning to My Father's Kitchen

Returning to My Father's Kitchen

Essays

MONICA MACANSANTOS

Curbstone Books / Northwestern University Press
Evanston, Illinois

Curbstone Books
Northwestern University Press
www.nupress.northwestern.edu

Printed in the United States of America

10 9 8 7 6 5 4 3 2 1

ISBN 978-0-8101-4839-0 (paper)
ISBN 978-0-8101-4840-6 (ebook)

Cataloging-in-Publication Data are available from the Library of Congress.

For my father, Francis C. Macansantos,

and Dr. Michael Adams,

my second father in Texas

CONTENTS

Returning to My Father's Kitchen

I take solace in knowing how to make my father's chicken adobo.

When my father died, his adobo was one of the many dishes he'd often cook for us that wasn't lost forever with his sudden passing. Fate gave him no opportunity to prepare for his departure; if it had, my father would have written down all of his recipes, would have stocked our pantry with essential ingredients and left instructions for my mother on where to find his sukis—the vendors who had earned his loyalty at the public market—for the choicest eggs, rice, fish, and meat. He would have shown my mother how to find the freshest fish and how to prepare a native Filipino chicken for a luscious tinola soup. He wasn't the kind of man who'd leave his family in the lurch—he had taken on fully the responsibility of caring for us, and it wasn't a role he'd readily abandon.

But none of us knew that death would come to him as early as it did. He didn't know what awaited him as he prepared merienda for my mother and himself an hour before he died. I can't depend on my mother to remember what they ate for merienda that afternoon; I can't force her to relive the details of the saddest day of her life. My guess is that my father made his favorite hot chocolate by melting unsweetened tablea in boiling water—whenever I imagine this process, I am brought back to afternoons spent inhaling the intoxicating fragrance of pure native chocolate as my father stirred the thickening beverage in its pot. Chocolate was good for the heart, he often told my mother. She suffers from hypertension, and so he was always worried about her heart. He watched what we ate so closely that we never saw his heart attack coming.

My father used chicken breast for his adobo because it was the leanest cut, and before he soaked the meat in a mixture of soy sauce and calamansi juice, he'd peel off its skin, trimming away whatever fat remained clinging to its flesh. "The skin is full of cholesterol," my father said, ever conscious of his health and ours. Two years after his death, I still find myself trimming away whatever fat the butcher has failed to cut from the breast, a habit formed from years of preparing the dish far away from home, always conforming to my father's admonitions against the dangers of fat. Doing so may not have saved him, and it may not save me either, and yet I slice off the tiny bits of fat anyhow, feeling enshrouded by a familiar sense of safety as I follow my father's instructions. Any deviation would feel like a betrayal.

I first learned how to make my father's adobo in 2010, when I was about to leave for graduate school in the United States. My father was concerned about my ability to feed myself in a foreign country, especially since I'd yet to learn how to cook. He taught me to make his adobo, guiding me through a step-by-step process. Half a kilo of chicken breast, trimmed of fat and cut into small cubes. Cutting the meat into tiny pieces would allow it to soak up the calamansi and soy sauce mixture as the dish stewed in the pan. Ten tablespoons of soy sauce, preferably Silver Swan (the best soy sauce in the world, my father claimed) or another Filipino brand. The Chinese brand Lee Kum Kee came close and was readily available in the United States, but the Japanese Kikkoman was not suitable—great for sushi, it fell flat when one used it for adobo. Half a head of garlic, the cloves peeled and thrown in uncrushed: I'd need an entire head of garlic if making this dish in America, he said, since their garlic wasn't as potent as ours. Half a fistful of whole peppercorns and three bay leaves. Calamansi, a tiny citrus fruit native to Southeast Asia, was what gave my father's adobo its full-bodied flavor: its tartness was nuanced and layered, rounding out the dish by complementing the salty, spicy, and tangy flavors of the marinade. Other Filipinos use vinegar to fulfill the requisite sourness of the dish, but not my father: he would patiently slice up the small calamansi fruits, picking out their many seeds just so that he could squeeze their earthy, full-bodied juice into his adobo. The trick wasn't just to balance out the saltiness of the soy sauce with the sourness of a complementing juice but to add something that enhanced this mixture of flavors while bringing them together. This was what ten tablespoons of calamansi juice did: it rounded out the dish's flavors, resulting in a single, explosive bouquet.

There was no calamansi in the United States, he told me. We'd spent five years living there as a family when I was much younger—five years of substituting cherished ingredients of our native cuisine with whatever was available in a foreign land. You'll have to use limes or lemons instead of calamansi, he told me. I'd have to make do with their one-note sourness. I remember him saying this with regret: my impending departure was painful, though necessary. As a writer himself, he knew how little opportunity our own country had to offer me. As a former expatriate, he also knew the losses I'd endure in order to accept the gifts other countries would offer to me. The Michener fellowship was my first big break as a writer; no institution in the Philippines was capable of providing me with the same level of support for my writing. It was imperative I leave my country to pursue it. As someone writing at the peripheries of the English-speaking world, such separations were necessary for me to fulfill my potential. My father understood this, which was why he set me free into the world while attempting to nourish me with home-cooked food even from afar.

When I make my father's adobo in his kitchen, years after our first parting, I patiently slice open, seed, and squeeze out the calamansi juice into a saucepan. The process is tedious and time consuming, but I agree with my father: the juice of this fruit enhances the overall flavor of the dish with its complex notes. My father died while I was living in New Zealand, just a few months shy of completing my PhD and returning home, the end to our prolonged separation. I am following my father's advice now to touch base with the motherland after spending years away. It is strange how his death forced me to heed his advice; I had resisted the idea of coming home for more than just a short vacation while he was still alive. But I felt unmoored after his passing, and I had to return to the earth my father had known to regain my bearings.

Back in my parents' home, I write and I cook. My mother still hasn't learned to prepare many of my father's dishes and depends on me, the daughter who spent entire afternoons and evenings with her father as he prepared meals, to remember how he made our food. In turn, I've had to depend on the internet to recreate some of his dishes, like his chicken tinola soup, and this I only got right after multiple attempts. I made the mistake of including parts of the chicken with their skins on and created a heavy, oily soup that failed to capture the light and fresh flavors of my father's tinola. It finally occurred to me, on my fourth or fifth try, that my father had only ever used chicken breasts for this recipe, skin and fat completely shorn. Further, the recipe I found online included sautéed onions, which I don't remember my father putting in, as well as fish sauce, which he avoided because of his gout. But I still include malunggay, or moringa leaves, which he swore by: the tiny leaves stick to my fingers as I pull them from their stalks, releasing a robust, tangy flavor into the tinola when boiled.

Many of the dishes I've made for my mother while living with her have been mere approximations of my father's cooking, but I manage to get his chicken adobo right. Perhaps I had to return to the motherland to properly prepare my father's adobo. After all, when I was living in America and New Zealand, I had to make do with the lemons and limes I bought at the supermarket, which supplied the dish's necessary sourness but failed to bring forth the unique earthiness of my father's adobo. It was an earthiness I was raised on and which I often took for granted in my childhood, and which was oftentimes absent from the many adobos I made while living abroad. Perhaps this was my father's attempt at sustaining the ties that bound me to our homeland, to make my palate yearn for the flavors it produced in abundance.

One small departure I've made from my father's recipe is substituting his favorite soy sauce, Silver Swan, with another brand, Marca Piña, to express solidarity for the workers at the NutriAsia factories, where Silver Swan soy sauce is made, who have risen up against deplorable work conditions. My father always supported workers' rights and would have likely done the same. I can imagine him growing to prefer Marca Piña, which, in my opinion, is the better soy sauce: it's tangy, just like Silver Swan, and possesses a certain fruitiness that befits the brand's pineapple logo. Otherwise, it's still my father's adobo, and it's a dish that my mother never tires of, no matter how many times I make it for her.

"This tastes just like your father's adobo," she tells me as she eats.

Her words comfort me, and as I eat, I come close to convincing myself that my father is still around to make this dish for us, somehow.

* * *

When I returned to the Philippines for my father's funeral, our refrigerator was fully stocked with items my father had bought for future meals. Leftovers from a large pansit canton he had cooked the day before he died sat on a shelf inside a Tupperware container. My mother nearly forgot about my father's pansit until she was about to throw out the boxed dinner my aunt had bought for her the evening my father was declared dead at the hospital. My mother had no appetite that evening, so the boxed dinner had remained untouched in our refrigerator. Days later, returning home the evening after my father's funeral, my mother still didn't want to touch the boxed dinner: whether it was because she suspected the food had gone bad or because it brought back memories of a painful night, I wasn't quite sure. Either way, it wasn't my father's cooking, and it wouldn't bring us comfort on our first evening without him. Rooting around in the fridge for something to eat, my mother found the Tupperware filled with my father's pansit canton, a stir-fried egg noodle dish to which my father added vegetables, shrimp, and shredded chicken breast.

I stared at the meal he had prepared, feeling confused and oddly comforted that he was still capable of feeding us after death. As we ate his pansit, I thought of how typical it was for him to prepare a Tupperware filled with food for us before leaving town for a few days. It was quite tempting to believe that his absence from our dinner table that evening was only temporary.

I was afraid of finishing the pansit, but at the same time, I craved the solace his food provided. How could we live without his food that nourished us and brought us together as a family, even across vast distances? A month before he died, he had given me a new, "no-fuss" chicken caldereta recipe he had come upon by accident while experimenting with ingredients—he coached me by phone while I attempted to make it in my kitchenette in Wellington. "I think he wants to go there and cook it for you," my mother joked, as my father kept issuing instructions about the amounts of tomato sauce and cheese I was supposed to use.

When we finally finished the last of his pansit, I felt the familiar satisfaction of having just eaten a hearty home-cooked meal my father had prepared. The reality of my father's death hadn't set in, and the comforting flavors of the pansit made me feel as though he hadn't left us. It was a sensation, perhaps a delusion, that I continued to hold on to as the dish lingered on my palate that night and as I began to cook our meals in the weeks that followed his funeral, before I returned to New Zealand to finish my PhD. I found myself seized by a frenzy in my father's kitchen: I knew that we couldn't just depend on neighborhood eateries and fast-food joints for our next meals; they'd never fill our bodies with the same nourishment that my father's cooking had provided. His cooking had brought us together as a family, serving as a quiet witness to our shared stories, jokes, and celebrations. Cooking became my way of defying the fact of my father's absence, of keeping him alive in our bellies. Perhaps it was also my way of confronting the abyss I encountered whenever contemplating his passing: in his absence, I cooked, maintaining the rhythm of our days by filling them with his food.

I struggled to remember how he made various curries and fish dishes. I had to teach myself how to gut a fish. But by sheer luck, my father had committed to paper his own pansit recipe after having been invited to contribute an essay containing a recipe to an anthology on Filipino food writing. If not for this invitation, my father's pansit would have been lost to us, since it is a recipe that is complex and difficult to replicate from memory.

Unlike the pansit commonly served at roadside eateries in the Philippines that's drenched in cooking oil and soy sauce and sprinkled here and there with pork and vegetable trimmings, my father's pansit combines a generous helping of fresh garden vegetables with the meatier flavors of lean chicken breast, mushrooms, and shrimp to create a light but flavorful noodle dish. Cooking my father's pansit is a painstaking process that requires soaking shredded chicken breast in a mixture of soy sauce and ground pepper, chopping an assortment of vegetables, peeling and deveining shrimp, soaking dried mushrooms in water to be used for boiling the noodles, and cooking this large, unwieldy mixture in water and soy sauce. Following my father's detailed instructions reminds me of how finicky my father was, how unwilling he was to take shortcuts in his cooking. Every pansit he cooked for us was like a poem he wrote: detailed, nuanced, and complex, a labor of love he refused to cut corners with. It took me several attempts before I was finally able to make pansit the way my father did, and when I succeeded, it felt like a summoning forth of his spirit.

My mother tells me that my pansit tastes just like my father's, and whenever we sit down to eat it, I feel as though we are conjuring my father's presence at the table. Eating becomes a spiritual act, a means by which our bodies connect with the invisible yet felt. I'd like to say it is a form of prayer, but I feel it's more than that, for the next world responds to our yearning by nourishing our bodies with my father's food. It is the only form of prayer I know in which my entreaties are somewhat answered.

* * *

My father was praised for his cooking by relatives and friends alike, though he'd tell us that the true genius in the kitchen was his mother, my lola Peregrina. When I was growing up, Lola Peregrina, or Piring for short, lived on the island of Mindanao at the southern end of the Philippines while we lived in Baguio, a few hours north of Manila on the northern island of Luzon. Among his siblings, my father was the one who moved far away from his parents as a young man, and I could sense his chafing against the distances that separated him from my grandmother whenever he prepared a meal for us that my lola had once perfected. "There was an extra something to this dish when your lola Piring made this, something I can never quite capture," he'd tell me as I sat at our kitchen table while he cooked. It could be a certain complexity to the sweetness of her pork humba, or just a special zing in her fried chicken. I could sense in my father's cooking an attempt to bridge the distances that kept him apart from his mother, whom he spoke of fondly whenever he cooked, whose laughter and nourishment had helped him survive his own father's physical abuse. Lola Piring passed away before the advent of social media and video calls, and even before she died, it was a challenge to get her on the phone. Long-distance calls were expensive in the Philippines, and years of bountiful eating had taken a toll on her health by the time I was a teenager, so phone conversations with her were rare.

My lola's cooking is legendary in our family. My father never tired of telling me the story of how Lola Piring had baked a chocolate cake for his birthday in a tin can set atop a small fire in their backyard.

They were poor, and yet she managed to find a way to bake a birth-day cake for her son without an oven and prepare a memorable feast without the resources of a modern, fully equipped kitchen. My father took his inventiveness in the kitchen from his mother, which doesn't surprise me. The circumstances surrounding his own beginnings as a cook were similar to Lola Piring's: my parents weren't making enough money as young college instructors to dine out, and so my father taught himself how to cook, relying on childhood memories to help him re-create dishes my lola once made.

But memory is indeed a fickle instrument, and like my father, I beat myself up when my stir-fry beef with French beans differs greatly from what he made, or when I try and fail to make his tuna escabeche. I recall him grappling with his memories as he tried to remember one of Lola Piring's secret techniques that would turn a regular dish into a magical affair. He often complained that he could never cook a particular dish as well as Lola Piring, but I think this wasn't the primary reason for his frustration: cooking, for him, was a way of summoning forth the past, of shoring up what he had lost when he left his homeland of Mindanao. Like him, I also try to reclaim what I have lost when I cook, and though I succeed in making some of his dishes, some of his recipes are lost to the ether. Our faulty memories aren't always capable of granting our prayers, of allowing us to recre-ate a dish that perfectly invokes the spirits of the dead. This fact sits uneasily with me as I cook.

* * *

A week after we buried my father, I began to prepare afternoon merienda for myself and my mother on a regular basis. I'd buy pastries or rice cakes and pair them with my father's favorite tablea chocolate, using the same brand of unsweetened chocolate tablets I assumed my father used for his final merienda. It was my way of sustaining the rhythms of our household that were arranged around his cook-ing, for I could not allow our days to fall apart in his absence. My father scheduled our days around food, a convenient way of bringing us together for nourishment and conversation, and the one meal he never skipped was merienda, or afternoon tea. This was the time in which we'd sit back and reflect on our days. Whenever I visited from overseas, my father would prepare merienda for me while my mother was at work, and as we sat in his kitchen, drinking his hot chocolate and eating heated pastries, he'd ask me about my life, my writing, and my loves while sometimes pointing out a rare bird perched on our guava tree, or mentioning a woman he had met at the public market who practiced hilot massage and could possibly treat his aches and pains.

He did not teach me how to prepare tablea chocolate; I learned the process from following the instructions on a packet of tablea I bought for myself at a Filipino store in New Zealand. I bring the water to a boil and lower the flame as I drop the tablets into the pot. I discovered through trial and error how many tablets are needed for two cups of hot chocolate (four) and how long it takes for the tablets to dissolve (around fifteen minutes). My father used a thick metal pot for making the beverage, but I prefer a smaller pot with a thinner bottom because it has a handle that makes pouring easier. It feels like a small betrayal, but I'm sure my father would understand. In his absence, I am making do.

My mother swears that I have the same patience as my father, which is why I can wait for the tablets to melt and disperse in the simmering water instead of preparing hot Milo, which is easier and less time consuming. But I have my own reasons for making this chocolate drink, one of which is my fear of losing touch with the memories my father left us with if I do away with this simple ceremony.

So far, it has worked: my mother and I have cakes and drinks in the afternoon, and doing so has helped us return to the normal cadence of our family conversations in which aimless talk is interspersed with jokes and laughter. Humor was such a fundamental part of my father's personality; it sustained him through personal tragedy, as well as the excruciating boredom of daily life. It was a trait he inherited from my lola Piring, whose joie de vivre was irrepressible and so inevitably found expression in her jokes and cooking. Through war, dictatorship, and a difficult marriage, Lola Piring had cooked delicious food and made her children laugh through their pain.

Cooking, for both my father and Lola Piring, was a declaration of love. And it is how I keep them alive in my heart, because their love can only die if I stop loving.

Little Girls

I never knew that guava trees could blossom, not until I spotted one tiny white flower nestled among the thick, hardy leaves of our guava tree on a balmy April afternoon. The tree had never flowered in its lifetime; my father had patiently watered it when it was just a sapling, bearing witness to its miraculous flourishing after it shed its first leaves, intimating a premature death. It had grown barren again before our country was placed on lockdown, and my mother and I had given it up for dead, but as the streets emptied and the air cleared, green nodules emerged from the tree's dry branches. These nodules turned out to be the beginnings of bright green leaves, lengthening and unfurling as doctors and nurses fought for our lives and their own in isolation wards. This unexpected greening felt like a gift as the city fell silent, held in death's quiet vise. But I didn't expect these new leaves to also contain delicate, white petals.

Like a deck of cards expertly fanned, the blossom's white petals arranged themselves around a crown of starry white anthers, and I jokingly called it a "little girl" to a friend in San Francisco I'd sent a photo to, who gushed at its image on the other side of the world. "This makes me tremble inside," he said, and I took this to be a good thing: for every trembling, it seemed, there was also release, a joyous bursting forth.

The next day, there were a few more white flowers, some unfurling in pairs, others emerging alone through the dense thicket of leaves. They beamed at me, little white stars, as I sat on our balcony in the mornings, reading books I'd never had the time or patience for until lockdown brought my life to a standstill. First Katherine Mansfield, then Eudora Welty—I found solace in the patient cadences of their prose. Like these two authors, our guava tree had taken its sweet time before unleashing on us its unexpected gift. Pointing out the flowers to my mother, I again called them "little girls": wearing skirtfuls of petals and crowned with starry white anthers, they were little princesses emerging from my father's guava tree to cheer us up as the pandemic wore on. The name appealed to my mother, who started looking out for them in the morning, stepping onto our balcony as the sun slid across the yard, catching quick glimpses at our tree from the kitchen window as we ate breakfast. Like little girls, we'd erupt in excited titters when we spotted a new girl, her petals perfectly arranged around her crown.

Perfect flowers have male and female characteristics, and so perhaps we were misgendering our new companions as we called them little girls, and yet, in our isolation, they allowed us a brief and fleeting chance to be children again. In the afternoon, we'd find white petals scattered on our roof or on the ground, and we'd look up to see some of our little girls skirtless as they held onto their crowns. I found myself reassuring my mother, who was constantly worried that this would be the last of the little girls, that more girls were on their way. I pointed out the buds breaking open, the girls about to burst forth.

May arrived with its afternoon thunderstorms, and I watched uneasily as our little girls exposed themselves to nature's indifferent wrath. Anxiety gripped me as the skies darkened, and true enough, the thunderstorms would come, beating down on our rooftops, refusing to spare the little girls. Despite the entreaties my mother and I raised to the sky to be gentle on them, the rain would scatter their petals all over our driveway, sparing only their soaking crowns, mere remnants of their morning splendor. Near the end of each downpour, my mother and I would emerge onto the balcony, halving an orange between ourselves, mourning the little girls whose petals lay scattered around the guava tree, while noticing, to our surprise, more buds bursting open, white petals patiently pushing outward to meet the clearing skies.

One night, I dreamed that our little girls' blossoming had been hastened to short, quick explosions in which they turned a sickly shade of green before shriveling and falling away. I remember begging them to stop, which only seemed to speed their withering, before I noticed the guava tree itself shrinking as it returned to the dry earth.

Hoping my dream wasn't prophetic, I checked on the tree the next morning to see if its blossoming had finally come to an end. More little girls had emerged, their blossoming too insistent, too ebullient, to betray a slow and steady withering. Bees hovered from crown to crown, and I wondered if they were the ones responsible for the sweet, woody aroma wafting toward me as I stood on our balcony. New buds with white tips reassured me of more impending arrivals, and I silently thanked the bees and the rain that fed the tree's roots.

My mother and I wondered aloud if the guava tree had blossomed when my father was still around, whether perhaps we'd simply been too busy to notice. "But your father took notice of such things," my mother said, while another cluster of blossoms bobbed up and down. "He was attuned to the small things, even when I wasn't." I think of the years I spent overseas, too far from my father to be attuned to how his heart was slowly giving out even as it gave him life, how it would one day explode without warning as southerly winds howled outside my Wellington apartment. I remember how I forced myself to keep working on the novel he'd believed in the day before I received the news, even as I sensed, without having yet been told, that the earth beneath my feet was giving way.

I think about how my father kept watch over the guava sapling when I was in high school, watering it even when it appeared to be on the brink of death. Could he sense that its death was still a long way off, that it would flourish, exploding in blossoms, long after he was gone? Maybe this is also his gift to us—a bouquet of little girls for his beloved wife and daughter, a heart divulging its truths long after a man's death.

Becoming a Writer

The Silences We Write Against

My father was many things when I was growing up in America, but I had to be told, before I was aware of it, that he was also a writer. A child only knows the obvious: that her father cooks all her meals, walks her to the bus stop on a school day, takes her to the library when she wants to check out a new book, reads to her as she falls asleep, watches *Sesame Street* with her, works at a high school cafeteria. While I lay on my stomach in our apartment's living room, watching TV, I sometimes noticed that he sat at the kitchen table, scribbling sentences in battered spiral notebooks. But I knew too little to assign meaning to this. Like much of my father's life, the hours he spent with his notebooks went unexplained.

I must have said something about my father, made a simplistic generalization of the roles he played in my life, because one day he brought me to my parents' bedroom and pulled out a briefcase from his desk drawer. I remember staring at the handle as he opened the briefcase, for it had been gnawed at, exposing the sticky rubber underneath its plastic coating. (We purchased almost everything we owned from yard sales.) Inside the briefcase were two rolled certificates. He undid the ribbon that held the first one, and said, "Back in our home country, I was recognized as a writer. Here is the highest award a writer can win in the Philippines." It was a Palanca Award he'd won for a collection of English-language poetry in 1989, two years after I was born and a year before we left for America. He unrolled another certificate on which his name was printed; it was another Palanca

Award, a second prize for a collection of poems. "It's been a struggle for me to make a name for myself here, but I wanted you to know that I was able to do that back home," he said, allowing me to spread the certificates on my lap. As I handed them back to him, I asked myself why we had to come to America, why my father had to leave behind the people who recognized who he really was, who gave him prizes for all those hours spent laboring quietly over his notebooks.

I had only vague memories of the Philippines, having been brought to America at the age of three. But my parents constantly reminded me that the Philippines was our home and that we'd someday return. You had playmates there, my father said, and if you meet them again they'll speak to you in Tagalog, the language you were beginning to learn before we moved away. In the Philippines, we have a female president, a kind and brave woman who helped us win back our freedoms from an evil man named Marcos. It's a better place now, and we'll be back, as soon as your mother finishes what she needs to do. The more my father spoke about the Philippines, the more it came to represent a promised land—a place to which I could escape from the cruelties of America and the adult world. In the Philippines, I wouldn't be placed in detention by my teachers without explanation, wouldn't be a primary suspect when a desk was vandalized or a ruler snapped in two. I imagined myself playing the lead in a school play in the Philippines, not just a supporting role like a villain's minion or a tree. If the Philippines was a place where my father won prizes for his poems, surely it was also a place where I would belong.

Our time to return finally came when my mother defended her dissertation and earned her PhD in mathematics from the University of Delaware. My optimism nearly matched my father's sense of relief as we sold our belongings, packed the possessions we couldn't part with in balikbayan boxes, and bade farewell to my parents' friends, many of whom were Filipino. At farewell parties, I'd hear them ask my parents, in worried tones, if they thought I'd be able to adjust to "life back home" once we returned. Did one ever have to adjust to one's home? I asked myself. But my father was insistent. America wasn't our home. We didn't belong there.

* * *

We landed in Manila in November 1995, three days before Super Typhoon Rosing made landfall in Manila Bay and nearly blew out the bay window in my aunt's living room. The air was as thick as water when we landed, and my head swam in the heat as we walked down the tarmac. The ground I walked on, holding my mother's hand tightly, didn't feel solid enough; we had flown over the waters of the Pacific for what felt like an eternity, and even if I was now walking on solid ground, it didn't quite feel like we had landed. The inside of the airport was dingy and run-down; brown men with dark hair like mine barked orders at each other in a harsh alien tongue as they hauled luggage onto wooden platforms for us to claim. My aunt and cousin met us outside the airport, where everything seemed damp: the hot air, my cousin's sweat-stained T-shirt, the palm trees that dotted the center islands of streets, fronds gleaming with wetness.

A man with a soothing American drawl spoke on the radio when we arrived at my aunt's apartment in Malate, and I learned from my aunt that the voice on the radio belonged to my uncle. As a cousin handed me a Hershey's chocolate bar, my uncle announced on air that his wife's sister and husband, as well as their daughter Monica, had just landed in the country. He then put on the song, "Welcome Back." When my uncle returned from his shift at the radio station later that evening, I couldn't believe that this small, brown, gray-haired man was the same person who spoke in a perfect American accent on the airwaves. But when he opened his mouth, the familiar sounds of America tumbled forth from his lips, reassuring me that the United States wasn't too far away and that the Philippines wasn't such a dangerous, unfamiliar place. I immediately warmed up to my uncle because he sounded like me and told jokes I understood. I learned later that he had received elocution lessons from the Maryknoll nuns who taught at the exclusive Catholic school he'd attended as a boy in Baguio. When I think about him now, I see him as a person who reminded me of America, the land where I'd spent my formative years, and whose company allowed me to acknowledge the uneasiness I felt, back in the land my parents called home.

My parents did not warn me about the poverty I'd see on the streets of Manila when we departed Malate, four days later, for the city of Baguio. Instead of apologizing for the frantic crowds fighting for space in rickety jeeps and buses, my father pointed out the rice paddies that surrounded us as soon as we escaped the capital in a van our aunt had rented for us. Our hometown was in the mountains, and as we drove up the two-lane highway that snaked its way through the Cordillera mountain range, the air in the van grew thinner and a comfortable chill set in. Tall pine trees with scraggly branches replaced the squat, leafy trees of the lowlands. In the days that followed, I accompanied my parents as they revisited familiar haunts. We weren't on the move anymore, and they couldn't afford to reject what they saw. Like them, I had to take the Philippines for what it was. If someone blocked the sidewalk with their potted plants or sari-sari stall, we walked on the narrow street, risking being sideswiped by a car. There was nothing else we could do; this was our country.

* * *

Things only got worse when I reentered the third grade in a private Philippine school. It was hard enough that my classmates bullied me in a language I couldn't understand. Nothing was explained to me; lessons were meant to be memorized, not understood. Our teachers tested us for our ability to remember certain terms chosen from chapters in textbooks, and they didn't seem to care whether we understood these chapters or not. I struggled academically, my grades plummeting. My grades only began to rise again in fourth grade, when I taught myself to learn by rote. It didn't matter whether I understood *Charlotte's Web* or not, and it was better if I didn't waste my time trying to dwell on what the book was about. As long as I remembered exactly what the gander told Wilbur the pig when Wilbur tried to spin a web with a piece of string, I'd get a passing grade. My teacher wasn't interested in what I thought about the scene. She never asked what I thought about anything.

Although I eventually made it back onto the honor roll, I remained unhappy in school. My teachers considered me smart but only because I muted my thoughts and dutifully repeated everything they said back to them. I retreated into books because they allowed me to think independently, to respond to scenes described to me on the page with my own emotions, my own thoughts, my own passions. Books asked me questions, solicited my opinions, and surrounded me with sensory details that encouraged me to touch, to feel, to explore. I felt invisible in school, but when I retreated into the pages of a book, I reclaimed my selfhood.

I started writing poetry the summer after third grade, a few months after we resettled in the Philippines. That summer, writers from Manila traveled to Baguio in groups to conduct their yearly writers' workshops for emerging writers. It was an annual tradition among writers from Manila, many of whom taught at major universities, to flee the humid, mind-numbing heat of the lowlands and hide away in the resort town of Baguio for a week or two to talk about craft with young aspiring writers. Many of these writers were my father's friends, and he often took me with him when visiting them at hotels overlooking pine tree reserves envisioned by the American colonial government nearly a century before. What initially struck me when I met these writers was how uninhibited and relaxed they seemed: the women dressed differently than a lot of women I saw on the streets of Baguio, while the men made off-color jokes about book titles and never seemed to hold back, whether talking about writing or life. Whenever my father met a good friend from long ago, there would be an easy, forgiving camaraderie in their banter. I craved such freedom, especially when I returned to school after the summer break and grudgingly succumbed again to the rules from which I'd briefly escaped.

My father showed a poem I wrote about a cat to the poet and novelist Krip Yuson, at the time an editor of the literary section of the *Evening Paper*. Krip published the poem in a special section featuring child poets. My father showed his copy of my published poem to all his friends, and although his enthusiasm embarrassed me, it also helped restore my self-esteem. I had the capacity to leave my own imprint on the page, and even if my schoolteachers never knew about my published poem, it existed, which meant, somehow, that my voice mattered.

* * *

Every summer, my father and I would make the pilgrimage to the Visayan college town of Dumaguete, where he was invited by his former mentor, Edith L. Tiempo, one of the first Filipino graduates of the Iowa Writers' Workshop, to panel at the Silliman University National

Writers Workshop. After these trips, my father complained to my mother about the workshop fellows, usually students from Manila universities studying with professors on the panel, who listened with rapt attention to everything their professors said in workshop sessions while ignoring the advice of panelists from outside Manila. He complained about how some fellows chattered away while he was talking. I saw how these writers from outside Manila read students' manuscripts with care, some of them locking themselves up in their hotel rooms to go over a story or poem more than once while their colleagues from Manila went out at night to grab drinks with their students. After all, these Manila writers were the editors of anthologies publishing the works of up-and-coming writers, and some of them had columns in major broadsheets where they could mention the name of a student whose work had impressed them. My father, and many other writers from the regions, could only offer advice, and I was to learn later on, as I embarked on my own literary career, that advice alone carries little currency among the Philippine literary elite.

* * *

I've heard many say that one hasn't made it as a writer in the Philippines until one has won a Palanca Award. It's easy to put one's faith in the Palanca Awards, since entries are judged blind, but as I struggled to build my reputation as a writer in the Philippines, I learned that I'd have an edge over other contestants if I was lucky enough to have a former mentor sitting on the panel of judges whom I hadn't antagonized, and who liked my work. When my father was invited to sit on the panel of judges for English-language poetry, one of his fellow judges identified the entry of a former student because he had read the poems in workshop, and he became the entry's strongest advocate when he found that one of the poems in the collection was dedicated to him. Years later, a poet friend writing in Filipino was told by one of the judges, after losing the Palanca, "You should've told me that you entered so that I could've made sure that you won a prize."

My father admitted to me that when he joined the Palanca competition in the 1980s, there were those who sat on the panel of judges who believed in his work and were perhaps instrumental in helping him win his awards. These writers weren't necessarily his mentors, but they'd seen his work in magazines and believed that his career was worth championing. One of them was a leading literary critic who edited anthologies often referenced by academics across the country. As a writer from Zamboanga on the southern island of Mindanao, my father needed all the help he could get from editors in Manila. When my father had a falling out with this critic and editor who'd previously championed his work, inexplicable things began to happen.

The managing editor of a leading commercial press in the Philippines stopped speaking to my father for unknown reasons, which puzzled him because she'd approached him at a conference just a few months before and told him how much she admired his work. Many of his friends who held positions in publishing houses were giving him the cold shoulder. His name, which used to appear regularly in anthologies, disappeared from newer editions. His work was no longer included in textbooks on Philippine literature. He was slowly and silently being edged out of the writing community, and because the community maintained a code of silence about such matters, he didn't know how to fight back.

* * *

I knew it would be difficult to begin my writing career without the appropriate contacts in Manila. Perhaps I felt a nagging sense of inferiority, an awareness that all the good schools were in Manila, that everything was happening in Manila while us hillbillies were being left behind. Throughout my time in Baguio, I had gone to terrible schools where learning by rote was the rule, and as I grew tired of memorizing instead of learning, my grades bombed. I withdrew into myself, waiting for high school to end so that I could leave my hometown and go to college at the University of the Philippines (UP) in Diliman, where I'd heard that professors cared about one's ideas rather than one's ability to recite terms mentioned in textbooks. Because my grades in other subjects were terrible, I felt that writing was the only field in which I could prove myself. It became my key to freedom. Books allowed me to contemplate uncomfortable truths that weren't recited at us in our Values Education classes or easily reduced to simple, digestible statements. There was freedom to be found in reading—in thinking, in guessing, in getting things wrong, in disagreeing.

UP Diliman is a large public university, and when the group of friends I'd acquired freshman year dispersed upon moving to different dormitories for our second year, I soon felt lost amid the sea of faces I swam among on campus daily. I remembered how at home I'd felt with writers when my father took me to writers' workshops and conferences, and thought that if I could find writers to befriend at the university, I'd feel more supported.

"Do you smoke?" and "Do you drink?" were the first questions I was asked when I approached the bench where the first university writing organization I tried to join officially gathered on campus. The girl who asked me these questions had dyed-blonde hair and tapped away the ashes of her cigarette as she spoke. She then asked me what my name was and gave me a bored, nonchalant look when I replied. It was clear that if I wanted to gain entry into the club, I couldn't complain about her behavior, or the behavior of other members. As an applicant, I had to tolerate their private jokes, act unaffected when I asked a question and was ignored, pretend it was fine if I said hello to the group and didn't get a response, grin and bear it when they assigned me a nickname I didn't like. I found out from a fellow neophyte who completed the application process that for their final rite, they were blindfolded, driven to Los Baños, and plied with alcohol until they passed out. She laughed while telling me about it, saying, "I make newbies do it, too."

The second university writing organization I attempted to join, founded a quarter of a century before my time on campus and boasting multiple National Artists for literature among its alumni, reopened for applications in my sophomore year. An administrator of our university's creative writing center told me that anyone who'd been published in a major magazine was considered a full-fledged member. Since some of my poems had been published in the *Sunday Inquirer Magazine*, I told the then president of this organization about my publications so that I could gain membership without going through initiation rites. After allowing me to sit as a member for two weeks, he took me aside, informing me that I couldn't be considered a full-fledged member unless I went through the regular process of applying for membership, which included a final three-day rite in the province of Batangas. "It isn't fair if you don't go through what we went through," he told me.

Connections are made in these clubs. Important alliances are forged, and young writers gain exposure through the literary folios they produce. Alumni of these organizations become professors, editors, critics, and cultural workers who possess enough power to make or break the careers of younger writers. Perhaps this is why members imposed demeaning requirements on so-called newbies seeking entrance into their elite circles. They knew they were powerful; they knew they could enact their childish fantasies and get away with doing so. Because I was unwilling to participate in demeaning initiation rites that had nothing to do with writing, I was shut out of the writing community at UP Diliman entirely.

* * *

But I was writing well, and this enabled me to win fellowships at several summer writers' workshops. I'd found a few amazing mentors, teachers who sought to understand what the emerging writers they worked with were trying to achieve in their manuscripts, and who worked hard to find solutions to the roadblocks that new writers faced. On the other hand, there were those who had rigid ideas of what constituted "good writing" and who approached student work with deep-seated prejudices, unwilling to exert the effort to appreciate different aesthetics and approaches to craft. Most of the panelists I encountered at workshops fell under this second category, doling out prescriptive advice or favoring work that was poorly written just because it echoed their political beliefs. Once, a panelist read my poem aloud in workshop and then read his altered version of my poem to the cheers and praises of panelists and fellows alike. Unsurprisingly, these were the panelists who, because of the confidence they exuded when they proclaimed their beliefs on craft and condemned what they perceived as failings in a fellow's manuscript, inspired the most respect. There were also those panelists with students among the fellows, or who had friends who mentored fellows in the cohort, and so dominated the conversation when those student's manuscripts were discussed. Months later, you'd often see the panelist's name on the cover of an anthology and the names of their mentees in the table of contents. The nepotism was disheartening, especially for those of us who already felt excluded.

Despite becoming more extroverted in college, I remained on the whole an introvert, and it was often difficult for me to connect with peers at workshops, to understand their private jokes, to penetrate the alliances that were forming. I didn't smoke, use their lingo, or drink much. I hadn't attended an elite private school in Manila and often didn't know the people or places my peers referenced. I had difficulty keeping up with their late-night drinking sessions, in which many of the panelists took part and where more connections were forged. At one workshop, I made the mistake of criticizing the work of an older fellow with strong social connections in Manila. Soon afterward, the entire cohort aligned itself against me, refusing to invite me to their parties, pretending I wasn't in the room when I was around, shooting down my comments in workshop, even remarking that a poem I submitted for workshop "wasn't a poem" at all. Shut out from their after-hours hobnobbing, it became a struggle for me to navigate the workshop itself. I wondered whether the panelists who hung out with the fellows on a regular basis knew what was going on, and I asked myself why they weren't doing anything to help. A few years later, a panelist confessed to me that he knew about what had occurred and that "he had taken their side," believing that I "didn't know how to deal with other writers."

But no amount of bullying from fellow writers could have prepared me for what I was about to experience at one particular writing workshop held yearly on the island of Mindanao. I had started writing fiction in my junior year, and the piece I turned in for my workshop in Iligan was the third short story I'd ever written. The panelist who was assigned to lead the discussion of my work, a respected academic from a university in Manila, was probably the only panelist at the workshop who was based in Manila—it was a workshop that prided itself on championing writing from the regions, and most of its panelists that year were academics from the Visayas and Mindanao. The panelist prefaced her discussion of my work by telling the group that "the writer of this short story will walk away from this workshop weeping" and that "five years from now, the writer will read her story again and cringe." Then she tore into my story, reading aloud a paragraph before noting that "elegant writing is out of fashion," declaring that my language was too florid, that people had stopped writing like Gregorio Brillantes way back in the 1980s. She criticized the subject of the story for being "too Filipino American," arguing that hyphenated literature was weak in content because it told the same story repeatedly. She spent the rest of the workshop session pointing out every detail of the piece that was not working for her, from a line that was "quotable" but "had no meaning" to the section breaks between scenes, which she insisted were "a marker of laziness." Even panelists who had initially pointed out the strengths of the piece started agreeing with her, while other panelists fell silent as she continued to pillory the story. One of the fellows, who later became a close friend, remembers a hush falling on the session hall when, upon finishing her lambast of my work, the panelist got up, walked up to the wooden stage, and waved her arms around and swayed her hips in a strange, awkward dance. I don't remember this happening, perhaps because I was too overwhelmed by her criticisms to notice. What I do remember was that she came up to me after the workshop ended, embraced me, and said, "You have no sense of literary language whatsoever. Face it, you're sophomoric."

As the week progressed and other manuscripts were discussed, I kept wondering why other panelists weren't stepping in to censure her for her behavior. She continued to bring up my work, often in the middle of another fellow's workshop, to point out its shortcomings and further highlight my story's failings. I was not her only target; she also tore apart another fellow's work, and after breaking down in tears, this fellow told the panelist that she hoped to enroll in one of her classes at UP because she had a lot to learn from her. The panelist spoke no further about the fellow's work in any of the sessions that followed this capitulation.

* * *

I returned to UP for my senior year a few weeks after the workshop, wanting to put my memories of the summer behind me as I immersed myself in my studies. I had planned to write a collection of poems for my undergraduate thesis, but after my experience in Iligan, I knew that if I stopped writing fiction for even just a few months, I would never write fiction again. And so I decided to write a collection of short stories for my thesis, switching over to fiction as my genre of concentration. For my critical introduction, I had to name my influences as a fiction writer, and I struggled with this requirement because I hadn't been reading fiction with the intent of finding models for my work. But then I had loved reading novels even before I started writing stories, and I could sense that what I enjoyed reading influenced my writing. Kawabata, James, Brillantes, Joaquin, Akutagawa, Tanizaki: they had been teaching me how to write when I was least aware of it. By drawing connections between works of fiction that appealed to me and what I wanted my own work to be, I was claiming an identity that was rightly mine and that one instructor had sought to take from me. Embracing the identity of a fiction writer gave me power, which perhaps explained why this woman sought to undermine my newfound identity at a national writers' workshop. As others told me later on, she perceived me as a threat.

As I was writing my thesis, I grew disillusioned with my coursework and the education I was receiving at UP. We were trained to depend heavily on literary theory when analyzing literary texts, and I oftentimes felt constricted by the theoretical frameworks I was forced to adopt. Writing literary criticism in my theory and literature classes meant finding a theoretical framework, which was either a school of theory or the ideas of a particular theorist, to use in our reading of a literary text. We were basically asking Foucault or Derrida to do our homework for us, and we weren't supposed to assist them in their work by sharing our ideas with them because there was no such thing as an original idea, according to my professors: everything was borrowed, they said, even our very thoughts. It was better to be honest about our thoughts, to admit that they originated from somewhere else, and it would be an act of plagiarism to even attempt to think on our own because that was simply impossible. I was beginning to feel as if I hadn't traveled too far from the schools in Baguio from which I fled. Learning methods at the university essentially mirrored the methods of my teachers in my hometown, but here we were committing to memory not only mere terms but entire chunks of ideas.

What surprised me was that many writers in the Philippines were quick to embrace these theories that negated the idea of Self and challenged the notion of authorship, claiming that authorship and selfhood were cultural constructs that limited their creative powers. It must have been freeing for them to think beyond the notion of Self, to surrender their authorship of a work of art and expect others to do the same. But I worry that the freedom one earns from this is merely a liberation from the responsibilities of authorship, the duty one has to take ownership of what one has written and to stand by its vision. There is also the freedom that comes with authorship, a liberation we earn when we take ownership of our words. It allows the author to assert their identity in the world through their work, to take a stand against those who seek to reduce them to compliant followers. Writing is liberating precisely because it is an act of will.

* * *

The belief that "there is no such thing as an original idea" is widely accepted in academic circles in the Philippines, and I've heard it repeated by many of my colleagues at UP Los Baños, where I taught for a few years after graduating college. It's a convenient idea to spread around if you're an academic wanting to dominate your students, or an established writer wishing to have a young writer's absolute loyalty. Once young people have their own ideas, they can assert their own identities. The bar is raised when artists and scholars are allowed to flourish on their own terms, and many do not want this kind of change.

Perhaps it was this desire to dictate the terms of my career that pushed me to apply to MFA programs in the United States. I'd never had a patron who championed my work and made sure that my name was mentioned in newspaper columns or was listed in anthologies that featured "the best young writers in the Philippines." For me, it had always been about the writing, and I needed the opportunity to focus my energies on honing my craft after spending so much time worrying that gatekeepers in my country would never open their doors for me.

I applied to six MFA programs, including one top-tier program, the James A. Michener Center for Writers at the University of Texas at Austin. Getting into the Michener Center was a long shot because they only offered twelve spots per year, and the year before I applied, they received more than eight hundred applications for these twelve spots (the year I applied, that number rose to more than eleven hundred). I was rejected by the other five schools to which I applied, and nearly gave up on my bid to get into an MFA program in the

States, even as I was put on a waitlist at the Michener Center. When I received my fifth rejection, I stopped checking my email because I couldn't bear to receive more bad news. I planned to quit my teaching job at UP Los Baños, move in with my parents for a year, and work my ass off improving my writing so that I'd have a stronger application to send to MFA programs the following year. I was on the bus to Baguio for the Easter break, and had just nodded off when I felt my phone vibrate. I took it out of my purse; my mother was on the other end. "Someone from the Michener Center called me and asked if I could get in touch with you," she said. "They've been trying to contact you for the past three days, but you haven't been answering their emails. They said they want you in Texas. You got in."

True enough, when I arrived at my parents' house at midnight, a note from Elizabeth McCracken was waiting in my inbox. "I know the Michener Center has been trying to get hold of you—and just wanted to add my voice to the chorus of people who would love to have you join us in the fall!" her message read. To have a writer whom I had never met tell me that I deserved a place in one of the most prestigious MFA programs in the United States, and for a manuscript that a renowned writer in the Philippines insisted was evidence that I "had no sense of literary language whatsoever" and was "sophomoric," was like being told that humans could fly.

Even after I had moved to Texas, I struggled to believe that I was talented enough to be called a James A. Michener fellow and to have a seat at a workshop table among other Michener fellows. During Cristina Garcia's introductory workshop for first year fellows, I couldn't get a word in during discussions—I had been away from America for such a long time, and I hadn't grown up like my American peers, who were so articulate, so confident about what they were saying, so well read. I had been told for years that my thoughts weren't valid unless they came from a book or were passed down to me from a professor. Even if I didn't believe this, I was nonetheless paralyzed with self-doubt whenever I opened my mouth to speak.

But my work was received well by my classmates, and this helped me regain my confidence. Writers in the Philippines often told me that we'd never gain acceptance from writers in America because they would never understand where we were coming from unless we exoticized ourselves. Though many of my experiences with the American publishing industry have shown me that there is some truth behind this sentiment, the Michener Center provided me with peers and mentors who received my work with enthusiasm, especially when my stories became more culturally grounded. At the very least, I was never forced to change my style and subject matter or conform to an aesthetic that wasn't of my choosing. I was, and still am, a straight-up realist who believes that the quietest of encounters can often be the most earthshaking and revelatory, especially since I have learned in life (and often through my dealings with the Philippine writing community) that silence is a weapon of choice among many. Our workshop leaders at the Michener Center, like Elizabeth McCracken, tried to understand what we sought to accomplish in our work and worked with us so that we could discover, on our own terms, the best ways to surmount the obstacles we faced. It was our work, after all, our statement to the world.

This isn't to say that I had no difficulty gaining acceptance from my mentors and peers while I was at the Michener Center. When I started writing stories about the immigrant experience, many of my classmates and some of my teachers complained that these stories had no conflict or that they didn't see anything wrong in a situation I presented even if they felt that "they were supposed to feel wrong." At times, I had to depend on my fellow writers of color to recognize and point out the sense of alienation that pervaded a scene, or the subtle acts of oppression in an otherwise ordinary encounter. The struggle for freedom shape-shifts when the enemy changes, but I am still here, raising my voice.

* * *

Many have said that our writing community is small because the Philippines is a small country to begin with. But our population is nearly twice the population of the United Kingdom and about a third of the population of the United States, which only shows that we aren't a small country at all. I'm beginning to suspect that our own exclusionary tactics are to blame for making our writing community as small and incestuous as it is. I'm sure that there have been many talented writers who were discouraged from pursuing careers in writing because of the blatant injustices they saw in the writing community—not everyone is born with a stubborn personality, like me. I've noticed that there aren't that many writers in the Philippines from working class backgrounds telling their stories, which makes me suspect that working class writers are easily turned off by the elitism of our writing circles. Perhaps we have made our own community an unwelcome place for many, which could explain why our work doesn't speak to our own people.

I haven't won a major prize in the Philippines or placed a story in a recent Filipino anthology. I'm often tempted to forget about the Philippines because I've had more success (though this too has been moderate) as a writer elsewhere. But I also feel that if I gave up on my country, I'd be allowing those who bully many of us into silence to win. The Philippine writing community isn't anyone's property, and I belong to it, as do many other writers whose names we have already forgotten.

For almost two decades we were made to believe that the Marcoses owned the Philippines, before we finally rose up to reclaim our freedoms. We sent a powerful family fleeing. My father insisted on returning to our country because he was optimistic that things would change for the better once the dictator was gone, freeing us to write our lives. When we returned, Filipinos had long gotten rid of the dictatorship, but not its ghost. That doesn't mean that we can't fight it, especially if it's just a ghost, a product of our own fears. I believe that a revolution can take place in the Philippine literary scene if we stop accepting the terms of a few who have been allowed to dictate the trajectories of our careers merely because they're good politicians. We are writers, not servants.

* * *

An earlier version of this essay was published in 2015, a few months before Rodrigo Duterte announced his candidacy in the 2016 presidential elections. As I am writing now, Ferdinand Marcos Jr. has been president of the Philippines for almost a year. I started writing this piece during what felt like a peaceful period in Philippine society, one in which an emerging writer like me could believe that raising her voice against rampant corruption in the literary community might lead to genuine change. Though I could sense that nothing much had changed in Philippine society since the fall of the Marcos dictatorship, I hadn't predicted that the return of authoritarianism would be as swift, and that it would take place merely a year after this essay's initial publication. To give credit to the literary community in the Philippines, many of its members were among the first to raise their voices against Duterte's violent war on drugs that claimed the lives of over twelve thousand Filipinos during his leadership. However, the community was also quick to rehabilitate the reputations of writer friends who publicly supported the killings. There has never been any coordinated effort to condemn writers and artists who have collaborated with both Duterte and Marcos administrations to whitewash their human rights violations. It takes great courage to condemn the actions of friends and colleagues, and yet our hesitation to take this necessary step is what allows authoritarianism to return to our lives in stealth.

I remember my time at the Michener Center with fondness, and I am thankful for the positive experiences I had there with my mentors and colleagues. Their belief in my work has sustained me through the many challenges thrown at me by a publishing landscape that can be particularly brutal for writers from the global south. I was immensely fortunate to have attended an MFA program that supported the kind of writing I wanted to do, and I understand that for many writers from non-Western or marginalized backgrounds, this is not always the case. It was at the Michener Center that I saw how established writers could be fair and generous to newcomers like me, and how my own hard work and artistic accomplishments could actually open doors. It was a life-changing experience, if one thinks about the world to which I had previously never quite belonged.

I Do Not Know How It Is
in Your Country

When we arrived at the address I had given to my university's international office, the young Chinese student who had been sent to welcome me and a few others at the Wellington airport helped me unload my bags from the van's trunk. I felt reassured by the emptiness of my new landlady's street, by the silence I had come to associate with safety and affluence during my three years of living in America. I had chosen to do my PhD in New Zealand on a whim, without knowing much about it apart from pictures of breathtaking landscapes I had seen on the internet, and I felt somewhat intimidated by this neighborhood of well-scrubbed streets and airy, glassed-in living rooms. And yet there was a pleasant crispness to the air, as though I were breaking through the clear, calm surface of a new life. The blinds of my new neighbors' homes were all drawn back, revealing couches and coats draped over their backs, almost as though these houses were all at ease with my presence, at least enough to disclose the quiet, private lives of their inhabitants to a newcomer like me.

I had been charmed by the Māori street signs I spotted on our way to my new neighborhood, taking this as a sign that the old and the new, the native and the foreign, coexisted happily in this country, or at least tried to. I was to learn that Karori, the name of this suburb, came from the Te Reo Māori *Kaharore*, an abbreviation of the Māori phrase "te kaha o ngā rore" meaning "the place of many bird snares." It was once a lush hunting ground for Indigenous Māori before European settlers arrived and leveled much of the native bush. Indeed, my landlady's living room had sweeping views of forested hills, and it was tempting to think that I had chanced upon an idyllic spot for my writing. My creative writing PhD program offered me time and support to work on a novel, but with only a rough idea of what I wanted to write, it was a project that filled me with uncertainty, just like the life I had chosen in this country where I knew no one. But could it be that bad, when I had already found a place to stay, a room in a light-filled house with a pleasant view? My landlady wasn't available to meet me, but she had left the key to her house with her next-door neighbor, a cheerful Malaysian woman who asked me if I was Filipino when she met me at her door. People had been nice to me during my first few hours in this country, and since my landlady had seemed kind in her emails, it felt unwise to doubt my good fortune as I sat in her sunny living room, glancing occasionally at a little dog sitting downstairs that barked whenever our eyes met.

Perhaps it had been this sense of willful optimism that allowed me to dismiss our student guide's misgivings when I told him how much I'd be paying for my room. "Does that include utilities and food?" he asked, after allowing an astonished silence to fill the van. Apart from us, there was a giggly Indonesian who furrowed his brows when I quoted the figures my landlady gave me and a distracted East Asian woman who remained silent throughout the ride. When I told them that my rent didn't cover utilities and food, our guide exclaimed, "That's too expensive!" before wondering aloud why we were venturing so far away from the city center. "We aren't in the city anymore, you know," he said, as high-rise buildings gave way to forested hills interspersed with Victorian homes. Having learned beforehand that everything in New Zealand was more expensive, I hadn't balked at my landlady's rent, especially since the room she was offering seemed large in pictures and had its own bathroom and private entrance. I had prepared my own meals and paid for my utilities while living in Texas and felt that the "bedsit" arrangement our student guide was referring to, in which a foreign student became part of a local family's household and paid a small fee in exchange for room and board, was somewhat infantilizing. After sitting in airplanes for nearly twelve hours, I felt as though I hadn't quite touched ground, and I brought out my American accent from its shelf, if only to prove that I wasn't as helpless as I felt. It was an accent I had acquired while living in Texas to avoid being questioned about my English fluency or my ability to belong, and in the company of these foreigners, I wielded it like a shield.

"Are there neighborhoods I'm supposed to avoid?" I asked our guide, who had already lived in Wellington for a year and had enough complaints about New Zealand to fill our trip from the airport to the suburbs.

"Just don't go where the Māori go," he replied, adding, "They nearly robbed me once."

"Is it okay to talk like this?" I wanted to ask, just as he began to describe how a group of Māori boys had tried to rob him after he'd withdrawn cash from an ATM. The Indonesian man erupted in titters, though whether it was to dispel our collective discomfort, I couldn't quite tell.

My landlady was a slight, graceful woman who taught at a local school, and when she arrived, she took me to my room and introduced me to her little dog, Eddie, who wagged his tail and followed us as she showed me around her house. She pointed out the framed pictures of her two daughters, one of whom was living in the United States. "You seem perfect," she said after we took our seats in her kitchen, where she told me I was welcome to help myself to her pantry before preparing dinner for us and opening a bottle of wine.

"To a new life," she said, as we clinked glasses. The warmth that rose through my body as I drank her wine reassured me as she talked about the differences between Australians and Kiwis, before mentioning her support for New Zealand's conservative prime minister, John Key. "We have what you'd call a tall poppy syndrome here, and people don't like that he worked his way up without accepting any help," she said. I had friends and relatives whose political views differed from mine, and so I chose not to assign too much meaning to her words. This woman had been generous to me, and on my first evening in a new country I was eager for good omens.

She and her daughter were up and about when I came upstairs for breakfast the next morning. Her daughter, a young woman who had just graduated from university, was as friendly as her mother and seemed excited to learn I was a writer. Inviting me to help myself to the breakfast they'd prepared, she talked about her older sister, who was dating a Stegner fellow and had given up her career as a lawyer in New Zealand to work for a nonprofit in America. Both she and her mother urged me to make myself feel at home, and in their company it was difficult not to. "My other daughter would love to know about you," my landlady said, as her younger daughter stacked our dishes in the sink. "She loves to hear about people from different countries."

Her daughter had left the kitchen when she added, "I don't know how it is in your country, but here we open the windows to let in fresh air." Caught by surprise, I didn't know how to respond. "We do that all the time in my country," I said, noticing how she was busying herself with the dishes, as though she hadn't heard me at all. "So Monica, do you mind if you open your sliding door just a little? Just to dry out your room," she responded, her eyes grazing my face.

I returned to my bedroom and opened my sliding door an inch, hoping to push away my misgivings to the farthest corner of my mind just as I heard a knock on my door. My landlady let herself in, holding a squeegee in one hand and a towel in the other. "Do you know what this is?" she asked, holding up a squeegee.

"Of course."

"The next time you take a shower, hose down the walls with the shower head, squeegee them, then use this towel to dry them off," she said, tossing them onto the bed. "I want to keep it clean."

She had promised to take me to their village, where there were two supermarkets and several banks. After I had showered and dressed, I returned to the kitchen, where she waited for me. "You take your time in the shower," she jokingly said, grabbing her purse from the kitchen counter. Sensing her meticulousness, I had done a thorough job of cleaning my shower stall, but now I wondered what it was, exactly, that she wanted. But my own confusion was silenced by her insistent footsteps as she made her way to her front door, and I hurried to follow her.

As we drove down a hilly road toward a cluster of shops she called their village, our easy conversation turned to the things I wanted to buy from the supermarket and the neighborhood public library that had a good selection of books. I hardly noticed when she parked right in front of an ATM—her morning cheeriness made me forget about my unpaid rent, and it was when she nodded at me that I remembered what our first order of business was.

She stood a few meters from me, watching me expectantly as the machine rejected my card. I panicked, for I had expected to withdraw the funds I needed from my overseas bank accounts before my scholarship checks came in. When I finally approached her to tell her what had just happened, her face darkened. "So you don't have my money?" she asked, her voice now a low growl. I rushed back to the ATM, pushing my card into the slot before figuring out that I had to withdraw smaller amounts from different accounts. Though astonished by her sudden hostility, I had no time to let it sink in—I was too afraid to displease her, for I had nowhere else to go.

She smiled when I handed her my rent and bond, and any misgivings I had were washed away by her good-naturedness as she helped me open a bank account and accompanied me to the grocery store. "You probably have so much more variety back home," she said to me, as we pushed our cart past shelves of fruit. I could sense that like many older white people I had met in the United States, her world remained small. It appeared like she was trying her best to welcome me into it, despite the strain my presence seemed to be exerting on its smallness.

The next day, a truck driver who sped past me while I was walking to the grocery store yelled something that sounded like "go home." Upon my return, I told her about what had happened, and she took me into her arms while declaring, "We love Filipinos here." It was the reassurance I needed to quiet my uneasiness over what had just happened, or what I perceived to have happened. I spent the rest of my day trying to cast aside its unpleasantness, determined to not let anything ruin the beginnings of what was a promising new chapter of my life.

The next morning, as I prepared my breakfast, she told me that her daughter in the United States was upset about the incident. "She's inconsolable," my landlady said, her voice gaining the heaviness of syrup. "She's mad that something like this would ever happen to you." I knew I was supposed to feel grateful for her daughter's sympathy, and yet her words pressed on me like an odd and uncomfortable weight.

Laughing, I said, "It's nothing." Her eyes remained pinned on me, and I glanced away from her as I poured coffee for myself.

"It's not nothing. It's terrible."

"Yeah." I was annoyed that she was bringing the incident up again; there was something about her exaggerated tone that made me squirm inside. Did she expect me to be unable to recover from it, when living in a body like mine made me a natural target for verbal attacks like these? Looking back at our exchange, there was something about the way she prodded the wound that makes me wonder if she was waiting for me to offer up my hurt, like a gift, to her.

But I wasn't yet willing to think of it in this way. I took a bus to my university, met my PhD supervisor for the first time, and took a tour of the campus and my new office with my institute's administrator. I sat with my discomfort until it slowly withered. I reminded myself that my landlady had insisted on taking my side, even as I tried to dismiss my own hurt. Her rage made me feel safe in a strange city, though it became increasingly friendly the more I talked to people and ventured down its streets. I bought ingredients for my dinner at a downtown supermarket and took a bus back home, only beginning to notice how quickly my expenses were eating into my savings when I got off at my stop and realized just how expensive my bus fare back to her house was.

She had welcomed me to use her pots and pans, and had taught me to use her expensive-looking range with prongs rising from a flat surface at the push of a button, emitting gas when I turned a dial. Encouraged to use her condiments, I twisted her Himalayan salt grinder over my simmering chicken, not realizing that the cap hadn't been screwed on tight. The cap fell into the pan, sending bright pink granules scattering all over my dish and onto the kitchen counter just as the front door opened and her lithe, assured footsteps announced her arrival.

"Is anything wrong, Monica?" she asked as she entered the kitchen, perhaps noticing the shock on my face as I attempted to gather myself.

"I'm so sorry. I accidentally spilled your salt." Glancing at the kitchen counter, I saw that I hadn't spilled that much, and was embarrassed at my own mortification—it was just salt, and surely it was nothing to her.

But then her face darkened, and in a low voice, she said, "That's very expensive salt."

She perched herself on a bar stool and folded her arms, her silence issuing an unspoken order as I gathered the pink crystals in my palm and poured them back into the grinder. Was this salt so precious that I had to pour it back into the shaker despite the dirt it may have touched? It wasn't something I would have done in my own household, and yet my movements were not my own as I felt her eyes watching my every move, pulling invisible strings attached to my limbs.

"That's enough," she said, as I tried to pick out more salt from my simmering dish. She narrowed her eyes and nodded as I apologized profusely.

In my room, out of her sight, my discomfort hung in the air like a low hum. I had seen the same salt at the nearby grocery store, and was sure it hadn't been that expensive. (True enough, a few days later I saw the same brand of salt in the supermarket being sold for about three NZ dollars.) I had lived in my own apartment prior to coming to New Zealand, and never thought I'd be reduced to a frightened child inside the place I lived.

I could hear her footsteps and then a rapping on my door. "You're in your room all the time. This is your house. Come out and explore!" she said, throwing her hands in the air. I smiled, thanked her, and told her I was busy attending to schoolwork. "But you can work in the living room too!" she said, her voice forming a gentle plea. Was she trying to apologize for what had happened earlier? I found myself softening to her, and my panic began to ebb as I picked up my laptop and followed her upstairs. She disappeared into the TV lounge right next to her kitchen, while I made for her living room overlooking the hills. I settled uncomfortably into a sofa, not knowing if I could get any writing done in this room that bore no trace of use. It was dark outside, and I could no longer see the hills outside the living room window, but the L-shape of the house allowed me to peer into its kitchen and TV room, where my landlady sat on an easy chair before a flickering screen. Was I a figurine in her dollhouse, to be bent and arranged according to her will? I had to admit that she had a way with me, and I returned to my room, hoping to get away from this queasy feeling.

The next day she saw me opening the pantry to reach for a canister of sugar. "When are you going to get your own stuff?" she asked, with a note of impatience.

Freezing in the middle of her kitchen, I answered, "I thought you told me to help myself."

"That's because you didn't have anything when you arrived," she said, her voice a sickly sweet caress. Glancing at the coffee I'd just made with her grounds in my small French press, she added, "Can't you buy your own coffee? That coffee is very expensive."

When I returned to my bedroom, I noticed that the bathrobe she had left hanging on my door had disappeared, and when I stepped inside what was supposedly my private bath, I noticed that the bottle of bodywash she had left for me was also gone. I was spending a lot of time in the shower, she said, when I stepped outside the bathroom. "Aren't you taking good care of that beautiful body of yours?" she asked, as I stood in her hallway with a towel wrapped around me. I didn't quite understand what she was getting at until she said it aloud: "But power is expensive, Monica, and with your tarrying my bill's shooting up."

I left for campus in a state of confusion. When I'd lived alone in the United States, I had been responsible for my food and utilities, and so this kind of arrangement wasn't new to me. I had known beforehand that my weekly rent only covered my lodging and nothing else, but my landlady had told me herself that I could help myself to their food, claiming this was included in my rent. With her invitation to help myself to her pantry came an invitation to belong, and I had banked on it as though it were an actual promise and not just an enticement to stay on. I was beginning to notice how much and how quickly my rent was eating into my graduate stipend and savings, but if I could use her condiments, make myself coffee, and help myself to an occasional egg, it was an arrangement that didn't seem that ungenerous. Without those things, I was beginning to feel cheated.

My office roommate, Therese, was at her desk when I opened the door to our shared office at the university. I sat at my desk and opened my laptop, hoping to begin work on my novel. But the words weren't coming, and soon I was talking to Therese. I learned from her that she had assumed I was an American because of my accent when we first met the day before. When I admitted to her that I'd only lived in the United States as a child and later for my MFA, she told me about her nightmare roommate at Iowa who threw dental floss and rolls of paper towels all over the floor, expecting Therese to clean up after her. Her candidness led me to open up about my own living situation, and her face colored in shock as I related to her the things I had experienced so far.

When I finally told her that my landlady adored their prime minister, Therese flinched.

"Oh my God. I hate her!" Therese exclaimed. "No wonder she's so awful."

"He's conservative, right?" I found strange gratification in her disgust.

"Yes, and they're like the Tories in Britain and conservative parties anywhere in the world," she said, crinkling her nose. "They're all greedy assholes who take advantage of the poor."

She then turned to her computer. "What's her name?" she asked, opening her search engine. "Is it this bitch?" she asked, pointing at a picture of a woman sharing my landlady's name. In her wrath I found a peculiar release—it was as if she had finally verbalized the rage I held in myself, but questioned.

"How much are you paying for your room?"

"Three hundred and fifty a week," I answered, "which doesn't include utilities."

"Three hundred and fifty a week for a room in Karori!" she exclaimed, aghast. "That's way too much!" She pulled up Trade Me, New Zealand's version of Craigslist. "I'm pretty sure she's overcharging you," she said, as she typed into a search box. "This, for instance," she said, showing me a garage apartment with its own entrance. "I know it's in a horrible neighborhood and you shouldn't live there, but look! You can get your own self-contained apartment closer to town for the same price you're paying."

I wasn't sure whether to feel angry for being duped or relief for having had my eyes opened to what I could already sense but hadn't had the courage to fully acknowledge. The Chinese student in my university shuttle had already pointed this out to me; why hadn't I listened to him? Perhaps having nowhere else to go had made me more willing to take my landlady's initial kindness at face value. Or did it take another white woman to tell me I was being swindled before I could finally acknowledge the glaring truth? Therese's outrage reassured me, and I found sanctuary in its power.

"If you want, we can drive around Wellington next Saturday and look at apartments," Therese said, pulling away from her computer. "I'm sure you can find something better than this. You look on Trade

Me for apartments that interest you, then we'll go visit them this weekend."

My landlady wasn't at home when I returned, and I used her condiments liberally as I cooked my dinner, hoping that the generous dashes of salt, pepper, and chili would help me somewhat recoup what she was overcharging me. When she returned home, she went straight to the kitchen and asked if I had used her condiments. I told her I hadn't, and when she slipped outside, I quickly threw another dash of pepper into my cooking.

"Could you clean up after yourself when you're done?" she asked when she returned. She sat on a barstool, pinching the stem of her wineglass. "I noticed a smudge on the gas range yesterday, right next to the prongs." I had thoroughly wiped down the range the day before, and wondered where, exactly, this smudge had been. Was she imagining things, or did she really expect her kitchen to be as clean as a showroom? I told myself that it wouldn't be too long until I found another place to stay as I wiped down the kitchen counters, spraying cleaning fluid right into the holes where the prongs emitting gas were embedded. I was afraid the fluid would seep farther down into the range's mechanisms, but it was what she had asked for, and I told myself that the consequences would be hers alone to shoulder as I shaped myself, like a pliable doll, to her ever-changing will.

"You're so domestic," she said, as she caught me cleaning her kitchen an hour after I had eaten my dinner. "Do you know how to use the dishwasher?"

"I had one in the States," I said, trying my best to disguise my seething. The word *domestic* hung in the air as I cleaned stains she herself had left.

A few days later, she asked me if I could leave the house for a few hours, since prospective buyers were arriving and she wanted the house to be spotlessly clean. (She planned to move to a smaller house, according to her emails, and proposed that I accompany her to her new home if I was willing.) She wanted me to fix up my own bedroom and remove my clothes from view, and before I could protest, she came in with a vacuum cleaner and told me to leave. She cleaned my bathroom after I had taken a shower and complained to me that I had left droplets on the walls. "But I squeegeed it down, and dried it with a towel," I said in disbelief, as she scrubbed nonexistent dirt from the crystal-clear glass walls. "How about this one here?" she asked, pointing at a minuscule droplet right near the door handle, hiding inside a spot that the squeegee couldn't reach.

I sat inside the neighborhood public library fuming. Try as I might to begin work on my novel, the words just wouldn't come. My land-lady was occupying too much space in my brain and body, and it was space I was not being paid rent for. Every day produced a new complaint: about the time I spent in the shower, about the minuscule droplets I had failed to wipe away, about the smell of my cooking "that clung to everything," about the burn marks I was supposedly leaving in her pans that only she could see, about how I was wast-ing electricity by switching on her dishwasher right after it had gone through one cycle (she had forgotten to put soap in the dispenser, and I had noticed how dirty the dishes inside were). I spent so much time in her kitchen, wiping away nonexistent stains and stains she herself had left while cooking. In her house I couldn't get any work done, especially since I hadn't been given a desk. When I asked for one, she told me to work in the living room where there was a coffee table, but I struggled to work in a space where she constantly peered in and asked intrusive questions. My bedroom wasn't off-limits to her; she was constantly knocking and peering in, and I often went to the university to get away from her needling. Even her dog's grow-ing fondness of me gnawed at her, for Eddie, whom she scolded for letting out the slightest yap ("Eedee! Eedee! Don't bark!" she'd yell, in her Kiwi accent), would approach me first, ignoring his mistress as she gave me suspicious, resentful looks. The space I rented in her house was not mine at all, and neither, it seemed, was my own body and mind; I carried her voice in my head wherever I went, and it was a voice that did not approve of me at all.

"Did you get any work done?" she asked, when I returned home.

"Not really," I said, too weary to put up appearances.

"Looks like it," she said, as she prepared dinner. I did a double take at her but couldn't read her blank face. Was she noticing things I thought she'd never observe, problems I thought were mine alone to worry over? Had she eased herself so deeply into my life that she could now criticize me for my creative paralysis, as if I alone were respon-sible for what I found myself unable to accomplish under her watch?

It was through small acts of rebellion that I found my life in her house bearable, for I couldn't stand the thought of giving her complete control. I savored my secret trips to apartment viewings, feeling a tingle running through my body like a furtive giggle that was mine alone to relish. When she wasn't looking, I'd dump her condiments into my cooking, and after she prohibited me from using her dishwashing liquid and asked me to buy my own, I'd pour her dishwashing liquid onto my dirty dishes when she wasn't paying attention. One morning, when she wasn't yet up, I made coffee with her grounds, and when she asked me where I had gotten my grounds, I told her I had used my own.

Her daughter told her that the gas range was beginning to make strange sounds, and they both wondered if it was because of the way I was cleaning it. Her daughter began reminding me not to store my food in the disposable takeaway containers they had once welcomed me to use. Knowing how her mother complained about the way my food smelled, even as I began to prepare blander, more Western food for my dinners, I wondered if she, too, was afraid to have their cheap containers contaminated by the things I ate.

"You do everything slowly, so I'm sure you'll be late for your coffee date," my landlady said to me one morning, as I prepared to meet a new friend. "I've been observing you. Your movements are so slow."

She chose the most inconsequential things to nitpick. She began to express alarm when I stepped into the kitchen to get something from the fridge without letting her know that I was in the room. "My goodness, Monica, you startled me," she said from her TV room couch, as I held on to the fridge door handle, trying to guess what I had done.

"It must be a cultural thing, to just enter a room unannounced," she added.

I closed the fridge door. "So what am I supposed to do?" I asked, confused.

"The next time you enter a room, could you please announce yourself? You startle people by just sneaking around like that."

I told Therese about the encounter the next day as she drove us into the city. "She just wants to bully you," she said, when I asked her if I had violated any cultural norm of which I was unaware. I decided to avoid my landlady as much as possible after that exchange, even when she knocked on my door, yet again, and told me in a syrupy voice,

"You're in your room all the time, and you never seem to be enjoying yourself."

"That's none of her business!" Therese exclaimed, as we made our way down Karori's main road into town. "Why would she care about what you're up to when you're paying your rent?"

In Therese's car, among scattered papers and cushions, I felt at home for the first time in a very long time. My heart was set on an apartment I had viewed the other day at the fringes of the city center—its occupant, a new divorcée with pink hair, tattoos, and a wry yet gentle sense of humor, was looking for someone to take over her lease. But Therese thought it would be good for me to have a look at other apartments I had seen on Trade Me, and as we drove across town, Therese told me the names of neighborhoods we were entering, allowing me to familiarize myself with a city that expanded before my eyes.

"I used to live there. That one's a shithole," she chuckled, as we parked in front of a house on my list. "I see they haven't even fixed it up. We can cross that one off your list."

She pointed at the weather-beaten houses facing the southern bay of Wellington and talked about how these working-class neighborhoods directly facing Antarctica bore the brunt of the southerly winds pushing their way into the city during wintertime. We lunched at a café near the water, savoring the ebbing warmth of a fading summer. As Therese went over the classifieds, searching for more apartments for rent, I thought of the foolhardy decisions I had made that brought me to this far edge of the world, how willing I seemed to bring myself so close to danger. But perhaps I was more prepared to handle these mishaps than I thought. As Therese talked about reading Mary Karr's *Lit* and how it reminded her so much of the working-class humor she grew up with, it occurred to me that I hadn't ventured too far from my comfort zone—that in places like this, there were people who weren't too different from the friends I had made in Texas or in the Philippines. I was far from home, and yet in the company of this woman who smoked, cursed out my landlady, and shared my literary tastes and politics, I felt like New Zealand, too, could become my home.

We spent the rest of the afternoon looking at apartments, Therese falling in love with an apartment facing the water while pulling me away from apartments I found decent or interesting because of a moldy smell or a suspicious chill that warned her of a lack of sunlight or insulation. "If I were you, I'd get the apartment that faces the water. It feels so dreamy, like you could get so much writing done there," she said, as we made our way back to the hills of Karori. It reassured me to have met someone who understood why I was here and what exactly would fill my heart with happiness.

My landlady was in a better mood than usual when I returned home, and as I sat in her kitchen eating dinner, she started asking me about my PhD and about the novel I planned to write for my thesis. "And what do you plan to do with it afterward?" she asked, in a voice that lacked its usual testiness. When I told her I wanted to teach and that I was thinking of returning to America, she said, "Well, with that American accent of yours, I'm sure you won't have much trouble fitting in." She asked me if my parents approved of what I was doing and added, "It's a nice thing to be doing now, but later on it might just be a hobby, you know, something you could do for fun."

"I don't plan to just do it for fun," I responded, and she nodded absentmindedly as I rose from my seat.

There was a long waiting list for the apartment overlooking the bay, but the apartment in town was still available, and the lady with pink hair was offering to pay half my bond and half my first month's rent if I took over her lease. I finally told my landlady that I had found another place to stay, and she accepted my announcement matter-of-factly, adding, "You seem to be unhappy here." Was she apologizing for the way I felt, or was she expecting an apology from me?

"Are there a lot of you living in that apartment?" she then asked.

"No, it will just be me." Did she expect me to fit into her image of an international student, sharing cramped quarters with fellow migrants even though I was already paying more to rent a room in her house than what I'd be paying to rent an entire apartment?

I wanted to move out as soon as I could, but she wouldn't return my bond unless I spent two more weeks at her house, which was what my bond covered in rent. She found a replacement for me a few days after I had given her notice, a lawyer from the UK her daughter in the United States knew who, like me, was coming to New Zealand not knowing what he was getting into.

"How unsurprising," the pink-haired woman said, as we met at my new apartment manager's office to sign paperwork. "It's the only kind of person she can fool."

My mother called me as I was cooking dinner that evening, and I stepped into the living room at the other end of my land-lady's L-shaped house to take her call. I stood near the window as my mother asked me about my new lease, sensing that my landlady, who had been sitting nearby when I stepped outside, would be up to something while I was away. As I stared through the living room window into the brightly lit kitchen, my landlady rose from her chair, approached the stove, and lifted the lid to peer at my cooking. "Sobra naman siya," my mother exclaimed when I described to her what was happening. "That's too much of her. You're paying rent!" My landlady sniffed my cooking, stared at it again, and then quickly replaced the lid. I returned to the kitchen where my landlady sat before her TV, never looking up to acknowledge what she'd done.

My mother discovered that she had friends from the Philippines living in Karori, and when they had me over for lunch, they were shocked to learn how much I was paying for rent. If only they'd known that I was coming to New Zealand, they said, they could have put me up in their spare room while I looked for more permanent lodgings. They offered to help me move to my new apartment and to lend me some used furniture they had retired to their basement. A woman who'd known my parents in the Philippines and was now living in Auckland rallied her friends in Wellington to help me settle in, and soon I was receiving free appliances and cookware, as well as invitations to house parties. Things were beginning to look up for me, but life in my landlady's house began to take a darker turn.

She began to complain of the hallway lights shining into her bed-room in the middle of the night when I switched them on to find my way to my bathroom. When I told her that I needed to use the bath-room, and needed the light to see where I was going, she snapped, "And I need to leave my bedroom door open to let the air in." After-ward, whenever I had to use the bathroom at night, I had to feel my way toward the bathroom in the dark.

I learned that the bathroom I was renting was not always mine, for she'd have Airbnb guests who'd stay in her master bedroom while she slept in her daughter's bedroom and shared my bathroom with me. Once again, she'd scold me for spending too much time in the bathroom and for not wiping every droplet off after my shower. I made the mistake of pouring myself a cup of coffee from the large pot she had made for her Airbnb guests, and when she noticed that the pot wasn't completely full, and that I was drinking a mysterious hot liquid from my mug that could only be her coffee, she hissed at me, "You will have to pay for that." Right at that moment, her Airbnb guests entered the kitchen, and her scowl was immediately replaced by a syrupy smile as she welcomed them in and poured them coffee.

I once returned from the university to find her in the kitchen, unwilling to smile at me when I greeted her, as per her request. When I went downstairs to use the bathroom, I noticed that the door was locked. I returned upstairs to see that she was gone. Eddie followed me downstairs and onto her deck, wagging his tail and watching as I pushed a deck chair under my bathroom window, forced the window open, and climbed inside.

My food containers vanished, and when I asked my landlady if she had seen them, she shrugged and shook her head. A few hours later, when I opened the coat closet to retrieve my jacket, there they were, hiding on a shelf. Had she locked the bathroom door on purpose, too?

She was strangely cheerful when I met her in the kitchen that evening, in stark contrast to her moodiness just a few hours before. "Did you have a wonderful day, Monica?" she chirped. I stared at her wide smile, which seemed to come so easily to her, and felt the ground beneath me shifting.

Even my facial expressions were fertile ground for her nitpicking. "Why don't you smile more?" she asked me one day, as I swept her kitchen floor.

I stared at her, bewildered. "Am I supposed to smile while cleaning up?"

"But I never see you smile, Monica, and I wonder why," she said, her voice turning airy and condescending. I had been told by friends and relatives that I smiled a lot, that I often smiled to myself without being aware of it, and her comment filled me with inexplicable rage. I wondered if she was gloating, having had a hand in my transformation.

The next day, as she prepared the house for another viewing, she asked me to vacuum my room despite its spotlessness. She carried her vacuum cleaner downstairs and deposited it in my room so that I wouldn't have a choice. "Carry it upstairs when you're done, would you," she said, turning away from me just as soon as she had appeared at my door. Behind closed doors I lay the nozzle on the floor and switched on the vacuum with my foot, letting it run without moving it.

To get away from her, I started taking walks to Karori Park at the opposite end of the suburb. It became a favorite part of my day. I loved watching the fog descending on the park's grassy field as I walked along its tree-lined circumference, nodding and smiling at joggers and dog walkers before I returned home. When she found out about my afternoon walks, my landlady said, "You never seemed like the kind of person who exercised." Then, as if remembering something, she added, "If only I'd known, I would have asked you to walk Eddie."

Even as she treated me like her maid, she continued to enjoy the financial benefits of my presence in her house. One morning I saw a new set of gaudy wineglasses arranged on her sideboard, beneath a pair of framed Marilyn Monroe glamour shots hanging in her living room without context or explanation. When she appeared, she ran an admiring hand over them, turned to me, and asked, "Do you like my new wineglasses?"

"They're okay," I said, unsure what she wanted me to say.

"They're from Germany, and cost two hundred and fifty dollars apiece," she said, in a childish, singsong voice. I stared at the wineglasses, asking myself if I could get away with knocking them over on purpose. But with just a few more days to go before my departure, I was too afraid to be held hostage by a woman who seemed to know no limits when it came to asserting what she believed to be hers.

That afternoon, as I was hanging my laundry outside, the Malaysian woman who lived next door waved at me from her balcony. Though we had never spoken to each other at length, we exchanged waves and smiles whenever she saw me through my landlady's kitchen window. She leaned forward and asked me if I'd like to come over for tea. I had wanted to speak to her for some time, and felt a quiet excitement as I told her I'd be ready in five minutes.

In her house she served me tea, and after we spoke about her children who were away at university and my own reasons for being in New Zealand, I told her everything I had experienced at my landlady's house. She listened to me in silence before talking about a young man who had once rented a bedsit in her house for much less than what I was paying my landlady. When I finally told her about the expensive wineglasses my landlady had bought with my rent, she laughed. "If you broke that mug, I wouldn't even care," she said, with a rueful smile.

She then rose from her chair, approaching the window before pointing at a large tree. "See that tree in our yard? She asked us to cut it down because its leaves were reflecting light into her bedroom. Do you notice those heavy curtains in her bedroom window? She put those up after we refused to cut it down."

I stared at her in shock. "What?"

She smiled and shrugged. She returned to her chair, took another sip from her mug, and said, "She used to give me her old *Woman's Day* magazines after she was done with them. She probably felt sorry for me, thought I couldn't afford to subscribe to *Woman's Day* myself, but I was okay with it. Then I saw they were having a competition where the prize was an all-expenses paid trip to Sri Lanka for two. So I cut out the coupon, attached a picture of me and my husband, and sent it in a few days before the deadline. Guess what?" Her face lit up with glee. "We won! I shared with her the good news, and from then on, she never gave me another *Woman's Day* again."

Perhaps this was what made my time at my landlady's house so confusing: the abrupt alternations between generosity and sadism, and oftentimes an odd, passive-aggressive combination of both. She could be kind to me as long as my actions did not threaten her peace of mind, but even the mere decision to retreat to my room was, for her, an act of rebellion. Her kindness was never unmixed with cruelty because it was the only way she could be kind: by currying my favor while also making sure I knew my place.

A few days later, my landlady knocked on my door to invite me upstairs to her daughter's birthday party. I didn't have it in me to reject what was becoming a rare generosity. To say no would be to displease her, and if there was going to be free food, then why not: I wasn't going to pass up the chance to recover some of my money.

Upstairs was her daughter, who sat on her boyfriend's lap as he ran a hand over her bare thigh and spanked it in full view of other guests; a chatty young man who, as I learned, was going to the United States with my landlady's daughter for their OE (overseas experience) year; a female friend of my landlady's who was talking about her recent trip to Sydney while showing off the brand-new blouse she was wearing, and two middle-aged men who started talking to me after we had been introduced. When one of them, a tall executive at a local IT company, found out that I had lived in Austin, he started telling me about his trip to Texas where, he realized, it wasn't customary to walk from one building to another in a sprawling, sweltering business park. "So you'll be taking the bus to uni," he said, when I told him I was moving into an apartment near the city center. "I haven't taken the bus in years. They never run on time."

It became apparent that this birthday party my landlady was throwing for her daughter also served as her send-off, since she was leaving with her friend the following month. A friend asked about her sister who was living in the States, and whether they'd be seeing each other. Excitedly, she and her mother started talking about her sister's humanitarian work, and about her recent stay at an artists' residency program in the United States, where she and her partner had worked on a film project about human trafficking in Southeast Asia. My landlady's daughter had seen some of it and was outraged by how poor families in "those countries" were willing to pimp out their children for sex. My landlady nodded in agreement, and her guests praised her older daughter for going all the way to Southeast Asia and risking her life on "those rickety boats" to help children.

I expected them to glance at me, their eyes drawn to my skin color and its implications. But instead they wallowed in self-satisfaction, bewailing the fates of these poor third-world children as though passing around a sweet, rich cake that nourished and filled their bellies.

"It happens in the Philippines, too, and most of their customers are Western men," I said, hoping to pop the thin bubble that protected them from the dangers of my presence.

The tall executive turned to me and said, "Yes, it's something the locals are used to doing to their children."

He then turned away, reentering a conversation to which I simply did not belong. I sat there in silence, my rage spreading through my body. My landlady's face was an unreadable mask as she continued to pour wine for her guests. Was their cruelty as thoughtless as it seemed, or was it my silence that they took for granted? I stared at the floor, seeing only the abuse I had been made to suffer through strewn all over my landlady's living room, like garbage they all expected me to pick up.

To Resist Being Unseen

On a rainy evening in June, I was walking from my apartment to a cocktail bar in Wellington's central business district, where a Meetup group I had joined was throwing a party. I had only been in Wellington for three months, and in a city where I hardly knew anyone, I was eager to make new friends. Despite the lengthening evenings and the cold, wet wind that signaled the beginning of winter, I was determined to get out of my tiny apartment and enjoy myself. It was two-for-one dessert night at the Library Bar, and I was in the mood to celebrate, since an essay that had been a personal struggle for me to write had just been published and was receiving positive reviews. I was keen to enjoy my success, even in the company of strangers—and being so far away from home gave me an added sense of liberation.

A strong downpour had eased into a drizzle by the time I set out, and I tailed a blonde in an athletic suit who jogged past me as I crossed the street near an intersection. There were no zebra crossings on this particular road, but there was a narrow "island refuge" for pedestrians where drivers were encouraged, but not required, to stop for them. In the middle of the road were two small protective curbs marking the island refuge, with a narrow passageway in between where pedestrians could pass. I decided to take this route to safely cross the street, seeing that other pedestrians, like the blonde jogging in front of me, were using it. It was still difficult for me to make the distinction between the different pedestrian lanes: in the United States, every pedestrian lane gave similar protections to pedestrians, and I thought it would be the same in New Zealand. My experience crossing roads in the United States, where drivers usually stopped for pedestrians even where crossings weren't clearly marked with zebra stripes and traffic lights, made me think that drivers in New Zealand would extend me the same courtesy. By the time a black car turned into the road, I was about to reach the protective spot between the two islands. I noticed the car turning just in time for me to hold up my hands and yell, "Stop!"

He stepped on the brakes, while I remained rooted in place, unable to move.

This is one detail that remains clear whenever I am compelled to recall that evening, even as time, and my own weariness, have frayed the edges of a memory that was once achingly sharp: in those seconds that passed before this man drove straight into me, I had decided, unconsciously, to stop in my tracks, trusting that whoever was behind the wheel had seen me and would not hurt me. It was the simple acknowledgment of my existence that I thought would protect me from harm, and it's the one detail from that evening to which my mind keeps returning whenever I try to make sense of a seemingly senseless event.

If he'd stopped when I held my hands up and screamed, that means he'd seen me.

When he drove straight into me afterward, I fell onto his hood. Pain seared through my shins as they collided against the hood's metal surface, and pain flashed through my hands as they slammed against the car's windshield. He stopped, then backed up, throwing me onto the ground.

As he pulled over, the blonde in sportswear who had been just a foot away from me turned and came to me. She and another woman who had been standing on the sidewalk helped me up. I could barely walk, but with their help, I reached the sidewalk.

"Are you okay?" they kept asking, as I limped between them. It was obvious that in their eyes, I was a victim, an injured girl worthy of their sympathy.

The driver was a middle-aged white man, and I noticed, as he stepped outside his car, that he wore what appeared to be an expensive pea coat. "I'm sorry. I didn't see you," the driver said, as he approached us. They turned to him, and the more he apologized, the more I could feel their sentiments shifting over to his side.

"In an accident, both parties are at fault," the blonde said.

"What do you mean?" I asked, disbelief shoring up instead of tempering the anger that welled up in me.

She avoided my eye as she continued to speak. "It's fifty-fifty, you know."

"You should have been looking," the other woman said.

"Isn't he supposed to look, too?" I snapped back, as my memory of those seconds before the collision reverberated. For hadn't he stopped when I yelled? Couldn't he have just waited for me to unfreeze, for my fear to dissipate so that my legs could move?

A wall was rising between me and these people who had helped me, and near them stood the man who had stepped out of his car. His car, whose metal shell had slammed into my bones. A car that could have killed me, if he had kept driving. As I hobbled toward a nearby wall and leaned against it, I could sense the suspicion in their eyes, in the uneasiness of their strained silence as I gave voice to my rage.

"I'm a pedestrian. I have rights," I kept saying, unable to believe that these people would so swiftly place the blame on me. I had done everything I could to follow the rules of law, but even this, apparently, did not protect me from blame.

A police car arrived. "Is this the person?" the constable asked bystanders as he paused to look at me. His hesitation struck me as odd: Why did he have to insist on labeling me merely as "the person," a strange term to use for someone who had clearly been injured?

"I have a name," I answered. I had already experienced more than a few incidents of discrimination that made me wary of the way the bystanders and police officer were treating me. As I stood before them, I began to sense that I was a merely a nuisance to these people, who seemed so eager to dismiss my pain.

* * *

I was rushed to the hospital in an ambulance and waited several hours in an emergency room lobby before a doctor saw me. While waiting, I called my mother's friend in Karori, who rushed to the hospital with her husband and sat with me while I waited to be treated. Past midnight, I was finally brought into the emergency room, and my mother's friend and her husband accompanied me as I was examined by a doctor. Despite internal bruises and external contusions, I had no internal injuries—concern sharpened the doctor's face when she turned to me and said, "You got off lucky." My mother's friend and husband thought it was better for me to spend the night with them, and in their son's vacated bedroom I slept fitfully—whenever I dropped off to sleep, I'd see a car driving straight into me. The next day, they brought me back to my apartment, where I began packing my bags for a temporary move to their house.

I could not spend another evening in my apartment, alone: I was afraid of going outside and crossing the street to buy food, and I was afraid that the dreams I'd have if I went to sleep, alone in my own house, would be much worse than the dreams I had the previous night in the house of my mother's friend. My knee and shin, which had hit the car's bumper when I fell onto its hood, had swelled, and my left hip and thigh were swollen, too, since they hit the ground first when I fell onto the street. My entire body felt tender to the touch as I moved around my apartment, figuring out what I needed to bring with me. I waited for a call from the police, since they had told me the previous night that they would be calling me to gather my statement the next day.

My phone rang as I was packing. It was the constable assigned to my case. "I am a strong woman," I kept telling myself. "I will tell my story without faltering."

"Bystanders say you were holding up a huge umbrella when you crossed the street that night. Is this true?" he asked.

I stared at my tiny folding umbrella, which I had used to protect myself from the rain as I crossed the street the previous night. I tried to wrap my head around the question he had asked. *Huge?* How could this umbrella be huge in the eyes of those who saw it?

It's fifty-fifty, you know. Both of you are at fault. Weren't you looking when you crossed the street?

"It's a small, folding umbrella," I answered.

"All right. Now, bystanders say that you were just two meters away from the moving car when you stepped onto the street. Is that correct?"

If I answered his question, would he allow me to tell the rest of my story? Or was my job to verify a story that others had finished telling for him?

"I don't remember. He could have been farther away," I said, not realizing that by saying this, I was already agreeing with him, that the moving car had been close enough for me to see when I stepped onto the street.

The rest of our conversation went on, just like this: with him supplying me with the supposed facts of the event, asking me to verify the details of a story he had pieced together before speaking to me.

"There are scientific studies that have shown that the memories of people directly involved in an incident are unreliable," I remember him saying, when I complained that I wasn't being given the opportunity to describe my own memories. "This is why we also depend on bystanders' accounts, because they can be more objective."

I remember interrupting him to say that the driver had paused for a few seconds when I held up my hands and yelled, only to drive straight into me. But he did not stop to take this in: instead, he brushed it aside, telling me to return to the narrative he had already written for me.

After wrapping up the conversation, he said, "This looks like a cut-and-dried case. Both of you appear to be at fault."

Hadn't he seen my injuries? Did he think I just rammed myself into this car? I was so far away from home, I told him, and to be told that I was at fault for something I had never asked for was too much for me to bear.

To this, he did not respond. He simply hung up.

* * *

My mother's friend came to pick me up, and as I ate dinner with her in Karori later that night, I received another call. This time, the man on the phone seemed gentle, even sympathetic: he asked me how I was and how my injuries were. "I was just driving last night, and I wanted to know how you are."

"Are you a witness?" I asked.

He paused, then said, "I was just driving."

It took me a few seconds for me to realize who he was.

"How are you?" he asked in a steady voice, as though he found nothing wrong in asking me this question, in calling me the night after he had driven his car right into me.

"You're the one who hit me," I said.

"No, I was just driving that night."

"Do you know how traumatized I am?" I asked, shaking, as my mother's friend glanced up at me. "I could barely sleep last night. What you did kept playing in my head, on a loop."

He giggled, and said, "That's not what I mean. How about your injuries? I mean, when you went to the hospital, did they find any injuries on your body?"

I hung up immediately.

"The nerve of that man! I would've thrown my phone!" my mother's friend said in Tagalog, as I tried to steady myself.

I learned, after making some calls, that the police had given my number to him, thinking it was perfectly fine to allow this man to contact me.

In the next few days, I consulted with a lawyer to learn how to stand up to a police force in a foreign country that insisted on erasing my story so as not to inconvenience a middle-aged, white New Zealander who was "just driving" that night as I crossed the street. I found the courage to go to Wellington's central police station and insist on delivering my own statement, without being interrupted. The officers at the station hesitated to entertain my request at first, since their colleague had already been assigned to the case, but eventually a female constable agreed to take down my statement. She took me into the station's cold, drab innards, sat me down before a desk, took out a pad of paper, and asked me to begin. She allowed me to tell my story in full, asking me, every once in a while, to clarify certain details. Afterward, she asked me, "What did this make you feel?"

Startled that she had even bothered to ask the question, I told her that it had given me much emotional distress. This, she also wrote down. I felt a deep yet unexpected sense of relief, for this was the first time that anyone had acknowledged that my feelings mattered and that they were, indeed, a vital part of my story.

A few hours later, I received another call from the police. Whoever was on the line wasn't the woman who had taken down my story, or even the detective who had spoken to me on the phone the previous day: he seemed to be a senior officer, judging by his brashness. I wasn't supposed to have gone to the station to deliver my statement, he said: my case had already been assigned to the officer who had taken down my statement on the phone the previous day, and it was the only statement they would consider. I was disrupting the investigation, I was told. Both the driver and I were at fault, he said, and no further action would be taken. He also added that the police had given my number to the driver of the car because both parties at fault in an accident were supposed to swap contact information.

"Is this the way victims are treated, by having their privacy violated?" I asked.

"We weren't violating anything. It's the law, and you're not a victim. You are equally at fault in this incident, and so it was his right to call you."

"But he hit me, and he injured me!"

"He did not hit you. Both of you are at fault in a traffic incident."

"But I was injured."

"You should've been looking."

"That sounds a lot like victim-blaming."

"You are not the victim here!" he yelled into the phone. "Stop using that as your bargaining chip. You are not a victim. You are equally at fault for not looking while crossing the street."

Though I am sure I did not hang up on him, I still cannot remember whether I fell silent, and whether he said anything more.

* * *

I learned that according to New Zealand law, once a police investigator makes a ruling on a case, nothing can be done to dispute their findings, no matter how faulty their investigation was. It was hard for me to accept that I had been silenced, that my testimony had meant nothing in the investigation.

I decided to file a complaint against the police with the Privacy Commission for giving out my number without my permission to the driver of the car. Afterward, I had to pack quickly, since I had a scheduled trip to the Philippines in a few days. I hadn't yet told my parents about the incident. They weren't the kind of parents who'd prevent me from going back to New Zealand once they learned about what had happened to me, but I was also their only child, and I didn't want to give them any more cause for worry.

I flew to the Philippines five days after the crash, still shaken from my ordeal. At airport security in Sydney, a woman in uniform and gloves asked me to step aside as I gathered my belongings from the conveyor trays. I asked her why. She told me I had to be screened for bomb paraphernalia.

"Do you speak English?" she asked me. This was after I had asked her why I was being taken aside, in perfect English.

As other passengers in my line, most of whom were white, walked past us, she searched through my bags, slipped her gloved hands all over my body, and asked me to roll up my T-shirt sleeves for further scrutiny. She asked me to take off my sneakers and smoothed a search stick all over them, the same stick she had used to rub my bare shoulders. I had received quick pat-downs in the past at US airports. This one went on for more than five minutes and was so thorough that I began to wonder if I had been singled out for any particular reason.

But do they ever confirm their true intentions to you, even as they run their suspicious hands and eyes over you, awakening an uncomfortable hum beneath your skin that never truly goes away? They never explicitly state their reasons for singling you out, for ignoring your perfect English, for erasing your story. They never call it racism. These men and women in uniform will tell you that they're doing their jobs, that they just want to protect you.

What they'll never admit to you is that they want to protect their own people from people like you.

After the screening was finished, I found a bench near the shops and cried.

* * *

When I returned to New Zealand a month later, I found a letter from the police in my mailbox. Whoever wrote my name and address on the envelope chose not to spell out my first name, preferring to address me by my first initial. They also couldn't be bothered to spell my last name correctly, which I only noticed years later, when I unearthed the envelope from my files while preparing to write this essay.

Despite having convinced myself that I had never looked at its contents, the flap came apart easily and without resistance, making me suspect otherwise. I had held on to all the details of the crash and its aftermath, so why did I have no memory of opening this letter or of reading it?

I understand now why my mind left a blank space, instead of a memory, in its wake when I first opened this envelope in 2015.

> Dear Ms. Macansentos [*sic*],
>   Re: MOTOR VEHICLE CRASH EVENT number—
> The vehicle crash in which you were involved in at the intersection of Taranaki and Abel Smith Streets, Wellington, that occurred on Tuesday the 2nd June 2015 has now been investigated and reported.
>   On reviewing the evidence we have concluded that we can not [*sic*] determine that one party is more at fault than the other and that the actions of both contributed to the crash.
>   There will be no further action.

Cannot determine that one party is more at fault than the other. The actions of both contributed to the crash. A flattening of an event that involved me and a man who rammed his car into me as I crossed the street. My mere presence on that street, apparently, *contributed to the crash.*

✳ ✳ ✳

New Zealand's Privacy Commission refused at first to investigate my complaint against the police, citing a law that required two parties involved in a collision to swap contact details. This was a misinterpretation of the law: I was not a driver of a vehicle involved in a collision, which would have required me to swap contact details with the other party, but a pedestrian crossing the street when a car collided with me. "Being the other party in the crash," apparently, had effectively ruled out my vulnerability as a pedestrian and had dismissed the amount of emotional hurt I had sustained by receiving an unexpected call from a man who had physically hurt me. The police had ruled out my rights as a pedestrian by misinterpreting the law, and it was when I pointed this out to them that they finally decided to pursue my complaint.

Two months after I filed my complaint with the Privacy Commission, I learned that the police had been found at fault for violating my privacy. A police officer called me after the Privacy Commission had made its ruling and said he wanted to apologize to me in person. He added that such conversations on the phone led to many misunderstandings and that he preferred to chat with me over coffee to get to know me better.

He wanted to get to know me. Did this mean he was also willing to listen? When one has been completely silenced by those in power, any gesture of kindness from them seems like an opportunity to unmute oneself, to resist erasure.

We met at my university's postgraduate student lounge. The barista froze when this gray-haired man in police uniform ordered two coffees for us. She then placed her hand on her chest and laughed. "Now this is quite the unexpected visit," she said, in the joking, neighborly tone I'd grown familiar with in the months I'd already spent in New Zealand.

We sat down after he paid our bill, and he proceeded to apologize on behalf of the officer assigned to the investigation. "He's a good guy, and he's sorry he made this mistake," the constable said, as he stirred sugar into his flat white. "But unfortunately, there's a small technicality with this privacy law," he said, grinning, "and so we have to admit to having made a mistake."

A small technicality. Had he come here to tell me that my victory was based on a small technicality?

"But of course it was our mistake, which was why I came here to apologize."

He held up his hands, as though in surrender, and grinned.

"Your laws are so messed up," I said. "In other countries, pedestrians are given the right of way. That street I was crossing had no pedestrian crossings, just an island refuge."

"Yes, but that's the law here, unfortunately. And you have the right to cross the street wherever you want, but it's also your responsibility to look for oncoming cars." He kept grinning, and it was difficult to tell what was on his mind.

"But shouldn't drivers also be responsible for looking out for pedestrians?"

"It's fifty-fifty. Both of you share responsibility."

"But drivers obviously have much more power than pedestrians, so their responsibility as drivers should be equal to the power they have," I said, in disbelief. "Pedestrians can't hit cars, cars hit pedestrians."

This was when he started interrupting me: the driver hadn't hit me, he kept repeating, but both of us were equally at fault. Exasperated, I said that he was participating in victim-blaming. He smiled again, and said, "You are not a victim. You are both equally at fault in this incident."

"I guess we'll never agree on this," I said.

"Remember that since you are both equally at fault, you are also responsible for paying the driver for damages if you dented his car," he added, with a smile.

This is another part of the story to which my mind keeps returning. I'd wonder, afterward, what this constable's purpose was in meeting me when he could have just apologized to me on the phone. Why did he need to say this to my face? Was it to remind me that despite my best efforts at resisting their silencing, I was just another object that could dent a man's car?

It seemed easier for me to fall silent, to forget it had ever happened.

"I hope this will be just another small, unpleasant event that won't ruin your stay here," he added.

Perhaps it was best for me to think of it that way.

* * *

Over the next three years I watched Kiwis jaywalk like nobody's business whenever waiting for pedestrian lights to change. Jaywalking was so common in New Zealand: people sauntered across the street as cars sped toward them, some running right in front of moving cars. I didn't dare risk it. This was their country, and these were their roads. They weren't mine.

I was nearly sideswiped as I crossed a quiet street corner near my apartment. Startled, I stared at the car that had sped around the curve without stopping and spotted the same driver inside the very same black car that had hit me just a few months before. Apparently, he hadn't mended his ways, but as the kind constable once reminded me, it was my responsibility to look.

I eventually started going out at night again, to meet new friends, to watch plays, to attend parties. I made friends who were native-born Kiwis, and they were sympathetic when I told them my story. I was beginning to live again, although sometimes my mind would return

to the passersby who had helped me up that night after I had fallen
onto the street, whose sympathies had immediately shifted as soon
as the driver stepped out of his car. Those people, just like my new
friends, had been kind; it took so little, it seemed, to lose the sympathies of kind people.

Nonetheless, I tried to live a normal life. I spent my first Christmas in New Zealand with a Filipino family in Auckland, and there I
fell in love. Vincent had immigrated to New Zealand with his family when he was a child, and like me, he knew what it was to be an
immigrant. While we shared a common cultural background, Vincent wasn't afraid to break free from its more restrictive norms. With
him, I felt more secure in a country that had seemed unwelcom-
ing just a few months before. As I made more friends and deepened
my relationship with this man, I began to feel that I was putting
down roots, to the point that I could almost call New Zealand
home.

But my trauma still trailed me whenever I crossed the street. Half
a year after the accident, I was afraid that if any of these drivers, who
never seemed to slow down when turning into the street, ran me over,
I'd be blamed, yet again. I had spoken briefly about the accident with
Vincent, and had told him about how afraid I was of Kiwi drivers.

"You're from the Philippines. Shouldn't you be used to bad driving?" he said at one point, perhaps when my complaints became too
much for him to handle.

Yes, I knew that drivers in the Philippines were bad—but I had
been hit by a car in New Zealand, not in the Philippines, and it was
in New Zealand that I had been told that I was at fault for it. "I was
at fault." The police had repeated this line to me over and over, until
I was nearly convinced that it was true. It was a line that stayed with
me wherever I went, for my existence in this country had already been
deemed a crime, an unwanted nuisance to those who truly belonged.

Was I being unreasonable for feeling traumatized because I was
from a third-world country where everything was supposedly far
worse? It seemed as if my boyfriend believed that I was complain-
ing too much, that I had no right to my trauma because of my
origins, which were also *his* origins. That we were supposed to be
more immune to trauma because of where *we* were from. We were
lucky enough to be here, he seemed to believe; to demand that our

humanity be recognized by these people was simply too much to ask from them.

One day, I texted him to say that I was terrified of stepping outside my apartment because I was terrified of Kiwi drivers. In response, he told me it was unfair to blame all Kiwi drivers for a mistake that one stupid driver made. That was when I finally lost it.

I pummeled him with messages comparing Kiwi drivers to American drivers, and New Zealand laws to American laws. I once lived in America, I repeated to him, and in America I never would have been held at fault for being hit by a car. Yes, I came from the Philippines where reckless drivers routinely ignored pedestrian rights, but this did not mean that I deserved to be blamed for what had been done to me in New Zealand.

In my rage, I failed to point out to him that I had been treated as a nuisance by bystanders and the police from the very beginning, or that the way in which the police had prevented me from delivering my full, uninterrupted statement made me suspect that they were prejudiced against me for one unacknowledged reason. All of the police officers I had dealt with during the investigation and its aftermath were white, and their dismissal of a key portion of my testimony made no sense, unless I acknowledged the possibility of racism. If the blonde jogger had switched places with me, would the police have dismissed her if she told them that the driver had first stepped on the brakes when he had seen her, only to drive straight into her?

It has since become clear to me how my outburst was directly related to my silencing. When my feelings of trauma were invalidated by the police, I was forced to keep my trauma hidden, and though it seemed invisible, even to myself at times, it never truly went away. It was why I saw the driver, the police, and the bystanders, who had also invalidated my victimization, in everyone I met in New Zealand. Since my victimhood was taken away from me, I was constantly primed for defense, not knowing what else would be taken away from me.

Perhaps Vincent understood this, for he called me from Auckland and told me that he was willing to listen if I wanted to tell him my story. And this I did.

* * *

In the months that followed the collision, I felt as though I were drowning. Try as I might to fight my way back to the surface, a weight pressing over me would force me back down.

Eventually, I learned to live with this feeling, to submerge it until it sat with me, like an unwelcome yet unobtrusive guest.

I took up yoga and Zumba, then started taking tango classes even though my left knee, which had sustained the greatest trauma from the collision, would occasionally buckle underneath me while I danced. I made more friends and traveled around the country. I allowed myself to be moved by the astounding scenery of my adopted home. The longer I lived in New Zealand, the more I felt a kinship with these people who had such a strong sense of community and wouldn't hesitate to help a neighbor in need.

Whenever people made rude comments about my country, questioned my ability to communicate in English, or made racist jokes about Filipinos and Asians to my face, I seethed in private but kept a straight face in public. I told myself that it was my foreignness that made me the target of racism, though Kiwis of Filipino descent told me that they were often subjected to similar racist remarks, simply because white, "Pākehā" Kiwis assumed that they couldn't possibly be New Zealanders, too. I learned that it was no use for me to raise a fuss: when I complained that my classmates' comments at a workshop were tinged with racism, I was disinvited from readings that were organized by a member of my PhD cohort, effectively shutting me out from the group. It seemed, during the rare occasions that I chose to call people out, that only I would suffer the consequences.

* * *

I returned to the Philippines after finishing my PhD and was preparing for another trip to the United States when I saw posts on social media about the massacre in Christchurch. I watched the news in shock. What kind of monster would want to destroy a beautiful community like Aotearoa, to inflict a deep wound on a nation that was bound together by trust?

I learned that the shooter had been living in Christchurch in plain sight of the police and had never been considered suspicious despite his online activities. That alt-right groups existed in Christchurch for years before the massacre, and the authorities had turned a blind eye to their proliferation.

During a memorial service at a mosque in Palmerston North, a man wearing a swastika-emblazoned undershirt was found loitering near the entrance of the mosque. On Radio New Zealand, a police spokesperson was quoted as saying, "The man was approached by the police. He was advised to move on and told that obviously what he was wearing at the time, considering what's happened on Friday, was inappropriate and yeah, basically suggesting that he move on—he complied and that was it."

A Muslim community leader spoke to *The Spinoff* in July 2020 about how their pleas for protection from the government, in light of increased vitriol from alt-right groups, were met with silence and inaction. How, instead of receiving protection from the government, their communities were placed under increased police surveillance. They weren't seen as people in need of protection but, instead, as people New Zealand had to protect itself from.

How much do our lives matter to you, when you insist on meeting our pleas, our complaints, with silence? Does our presence disturb you so much that you'd rather ram your cars into our bodies as we hold up our hands and beg you to stop, and shoot bullets into our bodies as we kneel in prayer?

The feeling of metal colliding straight into bone, of hands held up in panic before slamming into glass. My shortness of breath. My rage and grief as I slipped from that black hood and fell onto the ground.

I didn't see you, the driver said, as he stepped out of his car.

Then why the hell did you stop? I want to scream at him. You saw me, and then you refused to see me.

A Shared Stillness

I was a child when I learned from my father that his parents were once the tango champions of Zamboanga. I'd never met my paternal grandparents; I only knew what they looked like from pictures taken on their fiftieth wedding anniversary that my aunt Nancy had sent to us from the Philippines in a fat brown envelope. In these photographs, my lolo Manding is a thin, slightly stooped old man who never seems to smile, while my lola Piring is a small, plump woman whose easy smile is like my father's. In one photo, they stand side by side, my stern-looking, freckle-faced lolo Manding towering over my smiling lola Piring; in another, their blazing anniversary cake sets their figures alight as she feeds him a slice while he bends toward her, opening his mouth to receive her offering.

As we flipped through the pictures together, my father joyfully shared with me that my lolo and lola had been tango champions in their youth. In my mind, I saw a faceless young couple dancing in a dimly lit hall as a brass orchestra suffused their movements with a silent, metallic gleam. What did I know of tango? I was a child. I had seen Muppets from *Sesame Street* dance to the tune I associated with tango, its stiff, insistent beats knocking the smiles off their faces as they turned to the side, glancing away from their partners. I couldn't imagine my grandparents dancing to this tune—it was a song without warmth, incapable of filling their aged bodies with the vitality of youth. Because of course they had been young on that evening that had taken place years before, years before I was born, years before my father was born.

I was about to turn nine when I finally met my lolo Manding and lola Piring. Our family had just returned from the United States. My father brought me to Iligan, where my grandparents lived, nearly a daylong bus trip from their hometown of Zamboanga, a city they had left decades before. When we arrived at their one-story bungalow, Lolo Manding was sitting at the front porch, a frail figure in an undershirt and shorts who fixed a quiet, intent look on me as he exclaimed, "Monica!" with surprise. "That's your lolo Manding," my father said, as my lolo stared at me with his stern yet curious expression. He then turned away and slid a knife along the stem of a palm leaf in one swift motion, before placing it on a pile of clean, bone-white stems. He was making stick brooms out of these stems—a row of slim bundles, each tied together with a rubber band, rested beside him on the bamboo bench where he sat. Lola Piring was waiting inside, standing behind a table laden with food; she looked at me when we entered, exclaimed, "Monica!" and grabbed a small broom just like those Lolo Manding had made outside, using it to swat a fly with joyful flourish. "Ha ha!" she exclaimed, beaming at me. I was startled by her childlike glee.

When my cousins shut me out of their conversations, making fun of my cluelessness as I struggled to form words in Binisaya and Tagalog, I took shelter in Lola Piring's kitchen, her laughter and cooking making me feel warm and safe in a country I felt I hardly knew. She told jokes about hotcakes and the Macarena, listened happily to my stories about my playmates in America, and once in a while, danced alone inside her small living room. "Do you like to dance?" she once asked me, snapping her fingers to music only she could hear as it flowed through her body, loosening her limbs, rippling through her shoulders and hips like warm, gentle waves. She closed her eyes, tapping into memories she could not describe to me even in her good English. She welcomed the past into her body, banishing the years that aged her until even I could see her as a young woman, dancing to the rhythms of a faraway tune.

* * *

Years later, I'd find myself at a Mexican bar in Auckland, New Zealand, watching couples let loose with each other as they danced without any of the self-consciousness that held me back. I waited at the bar's fringes, wondering if I had it in me to join in, if all I needed was for a man to notice me and take my hand before teaching me how to execute such fluid, intricate movements. I watched the boy who had brought me to this salsa party as he shimmied and gyrated with other women. I felt strangely envious of these women, of their easy and fleeting intimacy with Vincent as they slipped into his quick embrace, trading flirtatious glances with him before spinning away, then spinning back into his arms.

"I really suck at this," I'd told him as he drove us to the bar in a city where I had only been for two days, in a country I'd lived in for less than a year. It was Christmas, but it was summertime in the southern hemisphere, and I was disoriented by the long days, by the heat that clung to my skin as I watched the women in tight dresses and men in thin cotton shirts work themselves into a sweat, their bodies radiating heat as they swayed together to the playful, insistent music. Not knowing how to dance, I stood at the fringes of the party, drinking glass after glass of water, wanting to leave even as I felt the music teasing me, pulling me in.

Finally, Vincent noticed me standing alone and wove through the throng of dancers toward me, leading me by the hand onto the dance floor as a new song began. I was relieved that he hadn't forgotten me, but I was terrified of looking like an ass after seeing so many graceful, beautiful women charm and seduce him on the dance floor. "Just relax," he said as he led me into simple salsa steps—back and forth, back and forth. I stared down at my feet, afraid of missing a beat. "Don't look at your feet, look at me," he said, and I must have flashed him a fearful look because he then said, "You have to trust me. Connect with me." His eyes were kind as he led me back and forth, side to side. "Notice how you're following me, without looking at your feet? That's called connection. Feel it." He spun me around and pulled me back into his arms, smiling as he caught me in a gentle embrace.

* * *

I never saw Lolo Manding dance like I had Lola Piring—not alone, nor with her. When I met him in Iligan, he was a quiet man who liked to sit on his front porch, smoking or making brooms, never speaking to me except on rare occasions, like when I once proclaimed at the dinner table that I wanted to be Japanese.

"Do you want to learn Japanese?" he asked me, peering at me through his thick glasses. "I know Japanese. I can teach you if you want to learn." I shrank back from this sudden invitation, embarrassed by the firmness of his tone.

Years after that visit, my father would tell me a story about how his father had, after noticing his son's failing grades, volunteered to tutor him in math. If my father made a mistake during these tutoring sessions, Lolo Manding would close the heavy math textbook, and with it, he'd smack my father on the head. Unsurprisingly, my father's math grades did not improve.

With people outside his family circle, Lolo Manding was never cruel; he was charming and warm, befriending Muslim tribal leaders on whose territories he sought to build schools and conduct anthropological research, delighting Japanese visitors to his schools with his fluent Nihongo, which he had learned as a young man during the Japanese occupation. He bonded with these men over drinks, the alcohol loosening him without hampering his ability to keep his violent tendencies in check. It was only when he came home, drunk, that he'd finally let his fury loose on his family, beating his children, haranguing his wife till morning.

When I was growing up, my father spoke candidly about the abuse he suffered at Lolo Manding's hands. At the same time, he shared many happy memories of his childhood, which oftentimes involved his mother, the jokester of the family, whom the children gravitated toward. My father latched on to Lola Piring's laughter as if it were a raft that could carry him away from the abuse, when actually it could only give him the fortitude to survive it.

* * *

"It's about letting go," Vincent said as he drove us back to his parents' home in the suburbs, his voice seemingly freed from its physical source as the darkness of the Auckland motorways enshrouded our bodies. "Which you did a while ago. Other women don't know how to let go, how to let the man take the lead, because they're used to being in charge. But you were listening. You were connecting to me."

Did I have to surrender to a man's will, make my body become a mere extension of his, to set my body free? It was a concept that disturbed me on an intellectual level, but when I'd danced with Vincent, I hadn't felt fettered at all—following his lead untethered me, allowing me to respond to his movements with a musicality that awakened to his touch.

He kept insisting that I was a good dancer as we exited the motorway, as we made our way down empty suburban streets. His parents were asleep when we arrived at their house. Vincent produced a bottle of wine and asked if I wanted a drink. His mother, who had known my mother in the Philippines, had invited me to spend the holidays with her family. I had met Vincent just the day before, on a rare evening he didn't come home late from dancing. We hadn't had a chance to talk at length before he had invited me to the salsa party at his mother's urging, and the wine allowed our talk to quickly grow aimless and intimate at once. When Vincent leaned forward to kiss me, it felt like the natural answer to a question that had lingered between us throughout the evening, freeing us both, allowing us to admit a simple truth.

We aimlessly drove around the working-class suburbs of West Auckland over the next few days, sneaking kisses in parking lots and public parks while his mother entertained guests and his brother prepared Christmas lunch. Vincent played tango music in his car as we drove past run-down bungalows, filling the embarrassed silence that fell between us whenever we weren't kissing with his knowledge about Argentina, where he had spent the previous year taking tango workshops, and the meanings of the songs playing, which were all about yearning and lost love. He loved salsa, he told me, but he loved tango even more—it wasn't just a dance, he said, and the more he struggled to describe it, the more it intimidated me. I mentioned to him that my grandparents had been the tango champions of Zamboanga, beginning to wonder if this was how they first met: an unlikely match with hardly anything in common, except perhaps a shared desire to be less alone. I had spent my first year in New Zealand without a partner, and while I'd made friends, it was still a strange country to me, made worse by racist remarks I had to parry from strangers and friends alike. Vincent, on the other hand, was a fellow immigrant who also confessed to having struggled to belong but who felt at home on the dance floor, among women who flirted with him as they surrendered to his lead.

"I should take you to a tango milonga before you go back to Wellington," Vincent said as the car slithered up the road that led to his parents' hillside home. We had only been dating for two days, behind his family's back, and I felt like it was too much. The way he spoke about tango made me feel wary of it, as if learning to dance it with him would solidify our status as a couple in ways I was not yet prepared for. Tango was a dance whose heartrending music Vincent played endlessly in his car, whose musicians sang and played their guts out. It was a dance asking for more than I was ready to give to this man I'd just met. Wellington was at the opposite end of New Zealand's North Island, an hour away from Auckland by plane and eleven hours away by land. Did he expect this relationship to go somewhere? "There's just something special about tango," he said as he pulled into his parents' driveway, switching off the car's engine before leaning in for another kiss.

✳ ✳ ✳

In the Spanish Creole they used at home, my father once wrote:

> You might have been handsome,
> But only if you kept moving,
> Only if you didn't stop to rest.
> If the spinning stopped,
> Your body looked famished, fallen in,
> *As though you had been shot—*
> Your cheeks sapped of their color.

Lola Piring's family belonged to the landed gentry of Zamboanga, and she had her pick of good-looking, wealthy suitors. Instead, she chose a man of humble origins, whose scrawny legs and sunken cheeks hid a violence that had taken shelter in his bones. She'd smile wistfully when my father and his siblings asked her why she'd married their father, whose bony frame bore no trace of youthful attractiveness. She always replied, "He was a beautiful dancer."

I can imagine how tango gave expression to their bliss, better than words: while language could cut and bruise, tango could soothe and forgive. "They didn't dance the same way people dance tango on TV," my father said. His parents continued to dance together throughout their marriage in times of quiet in which their happiness found a rare synchronicity. "There was nothing flashy about the way they danced. It was close. Intimate. Simple."

> But really, you were hard to hit,
> And that way you avoided being killed by the Japs
> So many people died in the World War,
> Even more died
> In the American invasion
> That happened long before.

I try to imagine my grandparents in prewar Zamboanga, before Japanese bombs destroyed its Spanish colonial buildings and left many of its inhabitants dead, before my lolo learned Nihongo out of necessity—to appease the new colonizers, who needed convincing that he was human and not an animal to be shot at, bayoneted, raped. Long before memories of the war filled Lolo Manding's body with a trauma he carried silently until it exploded from his gaunt frame as he struck his children or lashed out at his wife, he had been a young dancer who could take any woman in his arms and make her feel safe, responding to her moods by leading her into movements that gave form and expression to her desires. His family was poor, and he wasn't particularly good-looking, but did such details matter if he set Lola Piring's heart aflame as she surrendered to his lead, guiding him with the light that spilled from within her as they spun across the floor?

I picture them dancing in their living room, the years of abuse and unhappiness dissolving as they hold each other and find an old, fond connection that lives in their bones, just as the steps of tango do. The cruce, the giro, the ocho cortado, the americana, the sacada, the volcada. Did it take a single dance to reassure Lolo Manding that everything was okay, that despite his nightmares and flashbacks, he was safe here with this woman who forgave him all his wrongs? It is difficult for me to assume that Lola Piring forgave him for his violence, but perhaps, within the breadth of a tango ballad, she was willing to forget, to trust him yet again.

* * *

"The first thing to learn in tango is how to walk," Vincent said, as we stood facing each other in the middle of my tiny living room in Wellington. He raised his palms, pressing them against mine. "Your weight should be on the balls of your feet. See how that makes you lean a bit forward, toward me? Now push a little, but not too much. Feel that pressure? That's how you form a connection," he said, his face breaking into a smile.

In the months since he had first flown to Wellington to visit me, we had done things together that could be considered more intimate than this: we had cooked dinners, talked for hours on end, fucked. And yet there was something quietly intimate about the act of pressing our hands together—it felt like praying, almost, except that we were giving ourselves up to each other, not to God. As Vincent stepped forward, I stepped back, each of our bodies becoming a perfect extension of the other as we leaned into our connection, feeling each other as he found his lead, and I followed.

"If you're losing the connection, connect to my torso, feel my connection in my hands. Don't push too hard. That's right," he said as we walked back and forth in my living room. "That's it. You're getting better."

"Don't overthink it," he had told me at the salsa party. I repeated this to myself as he taught me how to walk in my living room, as we made love in my loft, as we talked about our plans—his intentions to move to Wellington so that he could set himself free from his parents, from the expectations of a city where he had spent all of his immigrant life. Months later, my tango teachers would tell me the same thing: if I kept overthinking my steps, my body would never be set free. Let him take the lead, they'd tell me, placing my right hand in my partner's left hand, my left arm around his shoulder. Close your eyes and allow yourself to feel.

* * *

I wonder if, on the evening they were crowned the tango champions of Zamboanga, my grandparents danced to Carlos Gardel's "Por una Cabeza," alternating between quick, exuberant steps and slow, sensual movements. Or maybe they danced to Osvaldo Pugliese's more dramatic compositions, sliding across the hall before Lolo Manding led Lola Piring into an elegant pasada, in which she slowly turned sideways and stepped over his extended leg. Perhaps Lolo Manding embellished his turns with elaborate boleos as Lola Piring surrounded him with sweeping giros, her footwork light and precise. I wonder if they danced in a close, intimate embrace, like dancers in Buenos Aires, or in a looser, open embrace, as they do in Europe. Did they dance to a recording, needle sputtering over vinyl as they spun on their feet, or to a live orchestra hired by city officials to play for such a rare and special occasion? Maybe they performed their winning dance in Plaza Pershing, right in the colonial heart of old Zamboanga, inside its large gazebo, where spectators and competitors encircled them as they pivoted around each other, my lola's leg lifting slowly in the air as she closed her eyes in ecstasy. Or maybe they danced inside one of the many Spanish colonial–era buildings dotting the city, the lights dimmed underneath a domed ceiling, Lolo Manding stepping away ever so slightly from Lola Piring as she leaned against him, her leg wrapping around his.

Lolo Manding had given Lola Piring reason to trust him as he led her into the intricate steps, reaching toward her and around her as he gave form to the light that shone within her. It was a feeling, perhaps, that never left her body, despite the disappointments and heartaches that followed. On the dance floor, Lolo Manding was capable of a Zen-like transcendence that allowed their hearts to meet. Why couldn't he achieve the same calm in real life? Did my lola hold on to her memories of that magical evening, during those moments when my lolo was unwilling to protect her from his own violence?

* * *

I never danced with Vincent after our first tango lesson in my apartment. In a phone call a few weeks later, he confessed that his feelings for me had begun to wane. He said it was difficult for him to maintain

a connection without physical contact, and with an entire island separating us, opportunities for this were few and far between. He told
me that when we FaceTimed in the weeks following our tango lesson,
he'd found himself faking his affection—that when he'd told me that
he loved me, he wasn't sure if he truly meant it. Talking to me, he
said, now felt like a chore.

In the months that followed this final conversation, I'd replay our
relationship in my head on a daily basis, trying and failing to convince myself that the man who'd said these terrible things and the
man who had wooed me feverishly in the months between the salsa
party and tango lesson were one and the same person. Friends told
me to forget about him, but my memories hung in the air like an
unanswered question, needling me as I opened his food jars in my
kitchen, or as I sat in his favorite chair in my living room, sipping
the expensive tea he had given me as a gift on his first visit to my
apartment.

I stalked his Facebook feed, looking for clues. I noticed that his
pictures with his ex—his former professional dance partner—were
back up; I had asked him to take them down when we began dating.
Vincent had said she'd returned to France two years before we met.
As I looked at their pictures now, noticing how their eyes were closed
in what seemed to be a shared bliss as they danced down the streets of
Buenos Aires, I thought of how he had mentioned her often when we
were together—how he'd tell me I'd done something that reminded
him of her or how he recounted that when they lived together, he had
once punched a wall during an especially bad fight.

When he wooed me with visits and expensive gifts, was he reaching toward the past, hoping to retrieve what he had once shared with
this other woman? Perhaps even Vincent didn't know the answer. My
guess was that he had come to me to ease his confusion and heartbreak, realizing later that I couldn't give him the answers he was
searching for.

* * *

Most of us in the large auditorium where this free dance lesson took
place were beginners, and almost all of my partners that day pushed
me too hard or held their hands too slack against mine, responding

to my body without affection or care. Was there another partner out there whose hands would give mine just the right amount of pressure, whose arms would wrap around me like a snug glove?

Once in a while, I'd be partnered with a professional dancer who'd tell me that I was pushing too hard, that I had to relax my shoulders.

"You're good," an elderly man who had been dancing for years told me. "If you listen to tango music at home, you'll get even better."

At home, I listened to an Astor Piazzolla recording I found on YouTube, thinking of how I was prodding a fresh wound by continuing the lesson I'd begun with my ex-lover. Our relationship had ended like an abruptly concluded dance in which we parted ways before the song's end, Vincent's presence lingering in my body without his physicality to guide me toward the dance's natural ending.

There was so much to learn about tango—how to stand, how to walk, how to pivot and "dissociate" the body's two halves, how to keep one's feet turned outward at every step—and the men I danced with at the group lessons I attended didn't have the mastery of movement and connection that Vincent had possessed in his body when he gave me my first lesson. Whenever I had an especially bad dance with a fellow student who treated my body like a rag doll by pushing and pulling at it, I'd go home and cry. But my instructors told me I was improving, and once in a while, I'd perform a full dance with an instructor in which I'd execute its complicated steps effortlessly, without prior thought. Afterward, my classmates would clap, some asking me if I practiced at home. I admitted to them that I never practiced, and some looked at me in disbelief. I was at a loss as to how *that* had happened, when in the midst of the dance, I wasn't thinking at all. I'd close my eyes and allow the music to flow into me, feeling my partner's lead. The rest, it seemed, was beyond my control: all I knew was that there was a light inside me that glowed, making my movements effortless as long as I honored it.

I admit that I longed for Vincent when I danced at milongas with men who couldn't connect with me, instead treating my body like a doll to be bent and shaped to their will. There were times when no man at a milonga would make cabeceo—that knowing glance across a shadowy dance hall that serves as an invitation to dance—with me, making me feel even more undesired and alone. Was it neurotic of me to immerse myself in a dance that constantly reminded me of a lover who had rejected me? I sometimes asked myself if this was my true purpose: to keep my memories of Vincent close, even if they were built on deceptions. To hurt myself repeatedly, with every milonga and pairing that went wrong, and to enfold my arms around my memories even as he repeatedly pushed me away with his silence.

And yet, when I found a partner who connected with me, I'd feel the light shining within me, giving my movements a buoyancy and grace I hadn't thought possible, not before I started taking tango lessons in earnest, not before that salsa party where Vincent first recognized my glow. I honored my light's radiance by giving myself up to the strangers who made themselves vulnerable to me as we danced. Whenever I found the perfect partner at a milonga, I felt transubstantiated, as though my body had freed itself from the confines of its own physicality, as I let myself go.

* * *

I can imagine how tango lifted my grandparents away from a world of disorder and heartbreak, bringing them together in a shared stillness that gave them the strength to survive a war and its attendant memories, as well as a difficult marriage. Lolo Manding may have been incapable of abandoning his personal traumas, but when he danced with Lola Piring, he could at least shed his outward defensive shell, becoming for the length of the dance open and vulnerable. Perhaps what Lola Piring found in him during these moments of intimacy gave her faith in the life she had built with him, that it, too, could be meaningful and joyful despite the violence with which she had sadly become entwined.

When my father learned that I was taking tango lessons, he said, "You're following in the footsteps of your lolo and lola." Though my father was not a professional dancer, he'd occasionally burst into dance at unexpected moments, making up steps in the privacy of our home or as we walked in front of a Japanese restaurant, bringing laughter to waitstaff who saw his gleeful wiggling. He didn't have the patience to learn the steps of a formal dance like tango, but I'm sure he carried his parents' musicality and grace in his body, reining in the violence he'd inherited from his father and sparing me from the abuse he had suffered at Lolo Manding's hands.

And after the war I was born,
I on whom descended the hand
Heavy with the weight of anger,
Sorrow and fear all mixed,
From a heart that would have simply perished
Had it listened to the voice of despair.
How many did they kill—who were those who died?
The beauty of Zamboanga
Disrobed and sullied, the flesh
Penetrated by the bayonet.
You woke up from this actual nightmare
And got up unburnt from hell—
And you danced.

It was a joie de vivre that sustained Lolo Manding through the war and its aftermath, one that found full expression when he danced with the woman he loved. Lola Piring's fortitude, on the other hand, was the kind that held fast to life's radiance, knowing that to overcome heartbreak, she and her children had to open themselves up to the delights life offered them, releasing themselves from the traumas that would only hold them back from experiencing the joys of the world.

* * *

When I packed my tango shoes and dressed up for a milonga a week after returning from the Philippines, where I had attended my father's funeral, maybe it was sheer recklessness that propelled me to dance despite the rawness of my grief. My father's death was sudden and unexpected, and I remained in disbelief that he was gone from this world. I constantly felt as if the ground beneath me were giving way, sending me into a never-ending free fall. Life went on without him, even if I desperately wished to bring it to an abrupt and comforting pause.

As I found a table at the dimly lit milonga and strapped on my tango shoes, I felt like I was succumbing to this hollow inevitability. My father was gone, I told myself. There was nothing I could do but dance around my pain.

I danced horribly that night. Unable to connect, I second-guessed my partners' moves as I executed my own. An old man with whom I danced a full tanda took me aside to tell me that I didn't know what I was doing, which was why few men had invited me to the floor that evening. "Don't you know my father's dead," I wanted to say, as he continued his litany of criticisms about my dancing. I cried when I returned to my apartment that night, feeling helpless and unprotected as I tried, and failed yet again, to navigate my grief without my father to guide me.

It took a month for me to return to the dance floor, the time I needed to cradle and swaddle the pain that wouldn't leave my body. Finally, though I was still grieving, I knew somehow that I was no longer afraid to let my defenses down with a partner, that underneath my grief, my light refused to be dimmed. When, at another milonga, the same old man who'd lectured me took my hand and led me to the floor, enfolding his arms around me, I knew that if I only welcomed his lead, we could both discard our past selves, merging with the music as we danced together.

As he pulled me deeper into the dance, an ease overtook my body, loosening me, setting my body alight. Did my grandparents see me as I danced? Here I was, in a country they had never visited, honoring their shared story of survival and hope, merging myself with it as I surrendered to its warm and sustaining current.

"You must have been practicing a lot since last time," the old man said, leading me by the hand back to my table.

"I haven't danced for a month," I responded, taking my seat as I watched couples chatter and laugh while waiting for the next tanda to begin.

As I sat alone, watching these couples dance, my body hummed. My father was with me and within me, and so were my grandparents—they were no longer on this earth, but their grace and radiance glowed from within my living, dancing body.

My Father and W. B. Yeats

My father was a regular listener of Jaime Licauco's *Inner Mind on Radio*, which aired in the evenings in the Philippines when I was growing up. I have distinct memories of Licauco's deep, velvety voice ushering itself into our bright kitchen as my father settled into a chair, having finished washing the dinner dishes. Sometimes, he'd invite me to sit with him at our kitchen table as the famous paranormal expert told a story about a woman whose late father sent her a message from beyond the grave through her son, or about a man who felt himself rising from bed before catching a glimpse of his own slumbering body from where he stood. "Didn't this happen to you once?" my father asked, referring to the time in high school when I had taken a strange, slow-motion tour of my own bedroom while asleep in my bed. He was convinced that I had experienced an astral projection, explaining the phenomenon to me with the same conviction that Jaime Licauco's voice carried as he interviewed guests on his show. Our staticky radio coated their tales of out-of-body experiences and ghostly apparitions in a grainy, reverential film, and my father would repeat the stories to me in awestruck tones, making sure that I was following along. Not once did I think of questioning my father or the old man who hosted one of his favorite radio programs. I was swept up in the current of wonderment that filled our kitchen, carrying us away from the ordinariness of the room where we sat. My father's trust in Jaime Licauco left no space in my heart for doubt.

What made Jaime Licauco seem less like an intruder in our household spouting nonsensical claims and more like a welcome guest at our table was his ability to talk about the extraordinary experiences of his guests as though they were usual occurrences to be expected in a person's life. His guests mentioned strangers who appeared to them before disappearing into thin air, messages sent from dead loved ones via strange and overpowering scents, and sudden abilities to levitate. No matter the tale, Licauco listened intently, then shared a similar story he'd heard from a friend or colleague before offering explanations for the events in question that made sense—if one was willing to believe. Carefully, Licauco dissected each supernatural event to reveal the interlocking mechanisms behind them, making them seem ordinary, a part of the everyday world, without taking away their magic.

My mother teased my father about the ease with which he accepted Licauco's explanations—she oftentimes found my father gullible, susceptible to charlatans on the street who would've swindled him of their life savings if it weren't for her vigilance. But there was an earnestness in Jaime Licauco's manner that made one believe he was sharing these stories not for personal gain but to help others make sense of the inexplicable events in their lives, the events that other people dismissed as mere flights of fancy. For my father, trusting Licauco meant opening his eyes to a world that was more magical than what most people were willing to see.

* * *

Two days after my father's death, I arrived home to see his notebooks and papers scattered around our living room. His reading glasses, mended with a paper clip twisted around the rim, rested with their temples spread out on the phone table, beside his beloved armchair where he wrote poems in the early hours of morning. He had just started a new collection of poetry, about friends who were long gone, and inside his most current notebook were the titles of poems he had intended to write, listed at the top of each page, titles like "The Campus of Walpurgis Nacht," "The Ogre (A Villanelle)," and "Good P.M. (Vincent Price)," followed by empty, ruled space. I stared at the blank pages, falling into the silences my father had intended to fill. My grief was bottomless, and the silences he left behind accommodated its shape.

Hadn't my father asked for ten more years as we walked home during my most recent visit, ten more years for him to commit his memories to paper so that his friends could live on in a world that had seemingly forgotten them? Seven months later, I stared at the notebook's pages, holding on to the promise of these poems' titles. My father's unrealized poems haunted me, and I waited for a sign, a knocking on the wall, perhaps—a continuation of the story he had hoped to tell before mortality's unplanned interruption.

* * *

In his memoirs, the poet William Butler Yeats describes one of his early encounters with the supernatural as the unexplained sound of a shower of peas being thrown against a mirror in a room where he and a cousin sat while vacationing in Ballisodare, in the west of Ireland. Not knowing the source of the sound, he asked his cousin to check the next room. But then he heard a loud thump on a different wall, one that didn't face the room where the strange sounds first emerged. Later that day, a servant heard footsteps in the otherwise empty house, and when he and his cousins went out for a walk that night, the cousin who'd been with him earlier that morning saw the ground under nearby trees blazing with light. Other apparitions confronted them as they walked past the river's edge: a brilliant light moving over the river; a man coming toward them before disappearing into the water; and then another, smaller light moving up the mountain slope of Knocknarea at a pace Yeats claimed was too speedy to be the product of human footsteps. Shortly afterward, Yeats took to wandering the nearby hills of Ballisodare, questioning elderly inhabitants about local superstitions, believing himself now awakened to the presence of the otherworldly. He writes:

> I began occasionally telling people that one should believe whatever had been believed in all countries and periods, and only reject any part of it after much evidence, instead of starting all over afresh and only believing what one could prove.

Like Yeats, my father believed that doubt was what closed us off from the spirits walking among us, from the messages that came to us in our dreams. There is something about the Irish poet's eagerness and regard for the unknown and unexplainable that spoke to my father's poetic vision, for he also sought to express the magic of the ordinary in his work. My father believed that there was more to our world than what is immediately apparent on its surface, and this belief found its fullest expression in his poetry.

To the young writers who came to my father for advice, he'd speak of the expansiveness of Yeats's poetry, of how his imaginative leaps of faith resulted in astonishing clarity and wisdom when questioning the joys and tragedies of the human world. When I wrote what my father identified as my first mature poems, in high school, he showed me an early Yeats poem titled "Aedh Wishes for the Cloths of Heaven":

> Had I the heavens' embroidered cloths,
> Enwrought with golden and silver light,
> The blue and the dim and the dark cloths
> Of night and light and the half light,
> I would spread the cloths under your feet:
> But I, being poor, have only my dreams;
> I have spread my dreams under your feet;
> Tread softly because you tread on my dreams.

Growing up in the Philippines, where the poetry we were taught at school was moralistic and ironclad in its interpretations of the human experience, Yeats's poem opened my eyes to how poetry could offer space for expressing my own apprehensions about myself and my place in the world. Its speaker's vulnerability resonated with me; he accepts his own limitations, knowing how his dreams are puny in comparison to the greatness of the heavens, even as he aspires to lay his dreams at the feet of his beloved. It is a poem that is aspirational in its admission of smallness, bearing the knowledge that one's limitations do not invalidate the significance of one's gestures but rather allow one to find one's place within the vastness of the heavens. Rereading this poem over the years has helped me be comfortable with uncertainty—to remain receptive to the magnificence of the world, even when its mysteries lie beyond my grasp.

Perhaps it was with a similar vulnerability to the world's magnificence that my father wrote a poem for me, years before my first encounter with Yeats:

> I see someone running
> In the dawn-soft light:
> A sunning child—her hand, cloudlet.
> And here (I say with my hand) is noon, warming yours.
>
> Even yet in this light: spume made flesh,
> Wonder and frank gaze.
>
> For something unexpected
> I seem to have waited long—
> You seem so instantaneous, so presageless.
> Message from further back than the void,
> You are tinted by it.
>
> Stay, sprinter,
> Teach me, teach each moment, time.

Three years after his death, I read these words again, staring into the void from which he saw me emerging. This is where I continue to seek my father, losing myself in a vastness that is both his absence and presence all at once. Must I depend on his words alone to give shape to my grief as it reaches out in all directions, grasping for his materiality? Might there be magic found in this poem he left behind for me, a secret incantation that could bring him back from the abyss?

* * *

In Yeats's memoirs, he writes:

> But I wished by my writings and those of the school I
> hoped to found to have a secret symbolical relation to these

mysteries, for in that way, I thought, there will be a greater richness, a greater claim upon the love of the soul, doctrine without exhortation and rhetoric. Should not religion hide within the work of art as God is within His world, and how can the interpreter do more than whisper?

Poetry enabled Yeats to find magic in ordinary situations, pulling back the curtain of everyday experience to reveal the presence of a higher power in the objects that surround us. His turns of phrase are like magical sleights of hand, taking quiet moments and turning them into agents of the divine. For instance, consider the poem "The Wild Swans at Coole," in which Yeats's speaker observes a flock of swans congregating at a lake at his friend Lady Gregory's Coole Park estate:

> The trees are in their autumn beauty,
> The woodland paths are dry,
> Under the October twilight the water
> Mirrors a still sky;
> Upon the brimming water among the stones
> Are nine and fifty swans.
>
> The nineteenth Autumn has come upon me
> Since I first made my count,
> I saw, before I had well finished,
> All suddenly mount
> And scatter wheeling in great broken rings
> Upon their clamorous wings.

The power of the swans' beauty evades all human comprehension as they float on the water, seemingly self-possessed. The speaker tries to count them, perhaps in an effort to make sense of their sudden and mysterious visitation, but he has no control over the creatures, and they scatter before he can absorb the full impact of their magnificence. The beauty of these wild swans as their wings beat against the air, carrying them away, transfixes him, and he's taken by the gracefulness of their movements, aware of a great power that possesses them and evades his understanding.

Unwearied still, lover by lover,
They paddle in the cold,
Companionable streams or climb the air,
Their hearts have not grown old;
Passion or conquest, wander where they will,
Attend upon them still.

Unlike the poem's speaker, the swans seem untouched by the troubles of the world. There is a constancy in their unwearied movements, and like the universe that encompasses all creatures, their "hearts have not grown old." Perhaps this sense of wonderment will allow the speaker to be renewed and healed as he watches the birds from afar, for he realizes how insignificant his troubles seem when compared to the inexplicable power of the wild swans.

By remaining perceptive and open to the mysteries of the world, Yeats could convey the quiet, elemental forces that found expression in a flock of wild swans striking awe in a human heart. This sense of wonderment was also what made my father a poet, allowing him the ability to surrender himself to the mysterious forces he perceived in his surroundings, and then to be transformed by them. It was a process he described in his poem, "Baguio Fog":

Fog,
You strange familiar,
You buffet me again,
Nudge me
With the moisture
Of past encounters:
The lake a hushed,
Live jewel watching,
The highway tree drowning,
Arms flailing,
Struggling
In your Christmas smother.

What is this privacy
We share, moist-lipped,
Eyed? You seize me

By the muffler,
By the heart,
Me, a private denizen,
Citizen with all my rights
Caught in this sudden rush,
The ghosts of pasts returning,
This hushed presence, I
Am immersed
In this immensity
Of an embrace,
Precipitately blessed,
So many times
At once
Reborn.

Poetry was a kind of prayer for my father. It allowed him to connect with the divine while remaining grounded in this world. As the critic Jamie James writes in his essay, "W. B. Yeats, Magus," Yeats's lifelong obsession with magic and mysticism was intertwined with the refinement of his poetic craft, and I see in both his poetry and my father's a desire to reveal the presence of the divine in the material world. James goes on to cite Kathleen Raine, who says, "For Yeats magic was not so much a kind of poetry as poetry a kind of magic, and the object of both alike was evocation of energies and knowledge from beyond normal consciousness." The magic my father and Yeats wield in their poetry does not conjure energies from thin air but rather reveals energies already present in our world that many of us fail to see. Maybe it was their acceptance of their own smallness that helped them sense the vast powers present in their encounters with nature and to articulate these encounters so successfully in their poetry.

Must I accept my own limitations as I read my father's poetry, knowing that my communion with his words will not bring him back from the dead? Maybe I should find comfort in how his words examine the unknown, for reading his poetry allows me to stare with him at the very mysteries to which he now belongs.

* * *

I spent the weeks after my father's funeral wandering our house like a spirit separated from its body, unable to feel the ground beneath my feet as I hovered restlessly over the world my father had left behind. I flew back to New Zealand three weeks after we buried him, still in disbelief over his sudden passing as our plane made its slow, lengthy descent into Wellington. The plane emerged through the clouds into a sunny afternoon, skirting past a swath of wind turbines whose blades moved in languid motion beneath a brilliant blue sky that felt as endless and deep as my father's absence. I noticed the water's strange gleam as my airport shuttle circled the various bays of Wellington and felt blinded by the sky's overwhelming brilliance. When I arrived at my apartment, I collapsed on the floor and cried.

I had brought back with me a copy of my father's final book of poetry, *Snail Fever*, and in the months following his death, I read and reread its poems, seeking companionship in his words while navigating the waters of my grief alone. One poem I kept returning to during those months was "Via Air," which he wrote after attending his own father's funeral:

> On my way to your wake, Father,
> I let my thoughts fall toward you down there,
> Where in a final absolute patience
> You wait—or do not wait.
>
> Up here, more than a world subsists:
> Moist behemoths sprouted from spores of the ocean,
> Rise and arrogate space.
> I'll wager these are built by elfin hands,
> Frantic and numberless.
>
> As I gain the upper air
> The white masses become a highway
> With no end in sight.
>
> There is no way of knowing, Father,
> How all that water and air are held together,
> Seemingly with so much love—fragile and vast.

The love my father had for my lolo Manding was complicated: his father was physically and verbally abusive, and he found his son, who did not excel academically, to be a disappointment. My father's yearning to connect with my lolo came later in life, for time gave him distance from the abuse, enabling him to see their relationship in a different light. He'd tell me about how, as a teenager, he rebuffed his father's overtures to go fishing, pushing his father away in those few moments in which he displayed tenderness toward his son. Writing "Via Air" was a way for my father to reexamine the love they'd failed to fully communicate to each other in life, a love that transcended distances both emotional and metaphysical and that, as my father felt in the air on his way to his father's funeral, was fragile and vast.

Sitting with his words as I longed for him in my Wellington apartment, I felt like I wasn't alone. The future was a highway on which he was no longer present, and yet it led me back to him as he longed for his own father who was no longer there. Could he truly be absent from my world if his words—if his love—continued to sustain me? His love was silent, and yet it was the one thing that kept me from falling apart.

What is it about being up in the air that makes our losses feel more acute? Does our closeness to the heavens remind us of our own mortality as we stare out the plane's windows at the nothingness that surrounds us? My father found solace in the sky's vastness, for it gave his longing room to breathe.

In "An Irish Airman Foresees His Death," Yeats pictured Lady Gregory's son and his good friend, Major Gregory, flying in the air moments before his death:

> A lonely impulse of delight
> Drove to this tumult in the clouds;
> I balanced all, brought all to mind,
> The years to come seemed waste of breath,
> A waste of breath the years behind
> In balance with this life, this death.

Up in the air on that sunny Wellington afternoon, perhaps I felt my own mortality more acutely; maybe it was akin to what my father felt as he flew to his father's wake, overwhelmed by the invisible force that seemed to hold the whole sky together, which could only, in his words, be love. Does confronting our own mortality bring us closer to life's magic? For Yeats and my father, it allowed them to transcend the ordinariness of life, to reach toward the secret force that animates the living. Both men realized in their poetry that there is a greater force than life itself, one which enfolds the dying as they merge back into the silence from which they came.

* * *

The evening before I learned of my father's death, I was jolted awake in the middle of the night, feeling as though the earth had tipped sideways. My loft bedroom was dark and still, yet I was immobilized by fear, keenly feeling my solitude as I sought reassurance in the dark. A wave of contentment and peace suddenly swept over me, and in the moments before I fell back asleep, I felt cradled by an unexplainable tranquility. In the morning, I saw my mother's missed calls, and when I called her back and learned of my father's heart attack, I could not believe he was gone. I had felt enfolded by his presence upon waking, and not even my mother's voice on the phone could fully persuade me of his departure from this world.

He had passed away in the Philippines shortly before I was jolted awake in New Zealand, and I became convinced it was my father who had visited me that night and had swept me up in his embrace. Nothing else could explain the overwhelming happiness that had washed over my entire body, dissolving my fear. In the following months, I told friends about that evening, and while some believed me, others were doubtful—their "if it consoles you" sowed doubt in my once-unshakeable belief in my father's visitation. And yet I knew I had felt his embrace that night, for only his presence could have eased me back to sleep after my body knew what it knew.

Around the time that Yeats was assisting Lady Gregory in her research on Irish folklore, he experienced what he felt was a sudden connection with the divine while walking the grounds of her estate, which he describes in his memoirs:

> I was crossing one afternoon a little stream, and as I leaped
> I felt an emotion very strange to me—for all my thoughts

were pagan—a sense of utter dependence on the divine will. It was over in an instant, and I said to myself, "That is the way Christians feel." That night I seemed to wake in my bed to hear a voice saying, "The love of God for every soul is infinite, for every soul is unique; no other soul can satisfy the same need in God." At other times I received fragments of poems, partly hearing and partly seeing.

The overwhelming sense of well-being I felt on the evening of my father's passing was instantaneous. Whatever feeling had jolted me awake and filled me with dread suddenly became insignificant in the grand scheme of things. I felt cared for by an invisible and comforting force. Maybe my faith will guide me back to that moment, when I believed wholeheartedly in its power. If I am to have faith in a world my father no longer physically inhabits, perhaps I, like Yeats and my father, must believe in its magic.

My father was a product of this magic, and so am I; he understood how our lives belong to a mysterious alchemy of forces whose workings lie beyond human comprehension. In "Return to Maryhurst," a poem he dedicated to my mother, he marveled at the greatness of the miracle of life, describing his vulnerability in the face of nature's power as a product of the universe's innate tenderness:

> We will not be able to endure
> The sudden presence of God.
> Perhaps it is distance and time
> That help us nurture, nourish
> All this tenderness, without which,
> After all, there would be no birth
> Of ecstasy, no exquisite pain
> Of heartache or of joy,
> Without which God would only be brute strength,
> Unable to suffer, uncouth to bliss.
>
> Why should there be so much care in the fashioning
> Of the tiniest things, the frailest threads
> That break, the subtlest of feelings—
> And why such power bursting in countless,

If meaningless intensities,
Stored in hearts that cannot
Contain them without perishing?
Why should, beyond this dying sun
Be only Space, the deluge of an emptiness,
The empty boast of emptiness?

This mysterious intensity that created my father also allowed joy and heartache and tenderness to bloom within him as he responded to the universe with an open heart, claiming his place within its vastness.

We will be taken, it is certain,
Though not without some surprise—
For as the years have shown,
The surprise has been mutual,
Surpassing most expectations,
The garden is still here, still fragile.
We are still here, still tender,
Ready for the taking,
Despite the slowly crumbling earth,
Despite the demanding sky—
Perhaps because of the sky,
To which we are a response,
For whatever it is worth.

Eastbourne, Wellington

A hush descends on the water, soaking through the darkness that has wrapped around me like a shawl. I bunch my shoulders inside my puffer jacket, wondering if I should have taken the 5 P.M. ferry back to the city instead of waiting for evening to completely seep through what is left of the afternoon. I am alone at the terminal, waiting for the 6 P.M. ferry, doubt coursing through my shivering body as I stare into the water's glimmering surface. Could there really be a 6 P.M. trip out of Eastbourne when I'm the only one waiting for it? The empty pier exposes me to the briny wind, and for a fleeting moment I am convinced that I am dreaming, which allows me to believe that a ferry is sailing toward me in the dark, journeying across the bay for its sole passenger.

My chin sinks into the soft new scarf I bought for myself just an hour before, feeling my neck grow warm inside its light and silky fabric. When I first saw it, looped around a coat hanger's neck inside a gift shop near the harbor, I was drawn to the warmth of its burnt orange hue. But after my fingers luxuriated in its softness, I looked at the price tag and hesitated. Thirty New Zealand dollars was a lot of money for someone who had just defended her PhD thesis and was no longer receiving a graduate stipend. The kind shopkeeper who puttered around me as I browsed explained that the scarf was made of wool and possum fur, which was what made it both warm and soft. Unable to brush aside her gentle charm, I told her I'd think about it—and when she said, "That's all right," I could sense that I'd be coming back.

Afterward, I found myself tightening my fringed acrylic scarf around my neck as I walked along the bay, the late afternoon wind whipping around my neck, slipping through my scarf's flimsy threads. Turning and walking to the other end of the bay, I lifted my scarf to my chin, following street signs that pointed me toward one of Katherine Mansfield's many childhood homes. I pressed on in the deepening dusk, my throat growing sore and my nose dribbling, as I searched for a house whose marker was nowhere to be found.

"It's a beautiful scarf," the woman said when I returned to her shop just before closing. "You can adjust the way it loops around your neck for any occasion."

It's warmer too, I reassure myself, fingering its dense weave as I wait for the 6 P.M. ferry. Matiu Island looms large and close, so different from the comforting, faraway speck it is when seen from the city. The only time I'd set foot on the island was with Vincent, who doled out grand but impossible promises while we ate our packed lunch. Now he is gone, and I am about to leave New Zealand for good. The city's faraway glow casts its soft net over the island, and I ask myself if this is the end, if it's truly time for me to go.

A speck of light encircles Matiu, and soon the light is sailing in my direction, assuming the outlines of a boat as it approaches. It cleaves through the silence with its mechanical hum, and then it is bobbing up and down beside me, disgorging its passengers, some carrying briefcases, some marching down the wooden walkway with headphones cupped around their ears. I wait for the ferry to empty out and then I step into its glowing interior, alone. The conductor nods at me when I take my seat and then slides the door closed.

The Power of a Vacant House

Gene and I hadn't seen each other in years when I heard of his mother's passing, but I felt I had to visit him when the news reached me. I hailed a taxi to take me to his house as soon as he texted his address, hoping my presence would bring him the same comfort I had craved from my friends as I stared in shock at my father's casket the year before. Perhaps I was merely trying to ease the loneliness I still carried with me after losing my father, for the rawness of my own grief gave me a sense of solidarity with those who were also experiencing it.

Gene and I went to the same high school, and though we weren't friends in those four years, we became friends on Facebook years later, when he reached out to me after I'd published my first short story in an American literary journal. Without the social hierarchy of high school imposing itself on us, we bonded over our love for books and writing, as well as our shared resentment for the teachers who hadn't nurtured our literary gifts. He confessed to me that he'd first noticed I was special when I delivered an impassioned report in our Filipino class that compared a chapter from José Rizal's *El filibusterismo* to a Rage Against the Machine song. "You were way ahead of us, which was why hardly anyone appreciated you," I remember him saying. In high school I had been made to feel unremarkable, even unintelligent, by teachers and classmates alike, and to learn that I'd had a quiet comrade during those years convinced me that, somehow, Gene and I had always been friends.

Opportunities to meet offline were few and far between. But we spoke every once in a while, sometimes to talk about his struggles

with the job market, sometimes to discuss how I would deal with
an erring boyfriend. He read my work and spoke about my stories as
though they were fascinating tales I'd told him over drinks. But we
both became busy with our careers and lives, and by the time Gene's
mother died, we hadn't spoken for more than a year.

I had just returned to the Philippines when I heard the news. My
grief, coupled with my fatigue from having barreled through the final
six months of my PhD while mourning the death of my father, had
landed me back in my hometown, where my mother continued to
mourn and I found myself adrift in a culture that now felt alien to
me. I felt at peace in my childhood home, reading my father's books
and reminiscing with my mother about his life, and yet I had not
expected to face so many difficulties reintegrating into the country
where I had spent the majority of my life. I struggled to make new
friends; it took some time for me to realize people rarely broke away
from their barkada, or group of friends, to form new friendships. My
old friends had either moved away or were too busy taking care of their
young families to spend time with someone they hadn't seen in years.
Gene was living in Manila, but when his mother died, he returned to
Baguio for the funeral. He was a friend, after all, and I thought it was
only right for me to pay Gene a visit at his mother's wake and to comfort him as he reeled from a shock that was painfully familiar to me.

* * *

The wake was held in Gene's home, which by all appearances, was
in a regular middle-class neighborhood like mine. I told myself I had
no reason to feel nervous about meeting Gene's family as the taxi
drove me across town. I knew, of course, that Gene belonged to a
prominent mining family in Baguio and that his family had once
owned the grand colonial-era mansion facing our city's central park
that had filled me with awe as a child. Painted a tasteful shade of rose,
it seemed straight out of a photograph from the American South. The
establishment of the American colonial government in our city in
the early twentieth century, and the arrival of American gold pros-
pectors eager to make their fortunes in the nearby mines, made it
common for houses like these to populate our city's landscape. It
was a storybook house built on the fortune made by one American

prospector who married an Indigenous woman. He chose the best plot of land in Baguio on which to build a home for his young family; it directly faced the city's central park designed by no less than Daniel Burnham. The three-story colonial revival mansion, with its arched porticos, sweeping balustrades, and Greek columns supporting an arched pediment that bore the family's initial, was visible to any ordinary citizen of Baguio taking a stroll through Burnham Park. It was a mansion designed to advertise its owner's wealth and cement his family's status in a fledgling colonial metropolis.

In high school, I'd known somehow that Gene belonged to a prominent family, though I only made the connection between his middle name and the fairy-tale mansion facing Burnham Park when he told me about how it had swayed, like a ship taking the beatings of a storm, when what became known as the Baguio earthquake hit our city in 1990. Apart from this incident, he said, he'd spent an otherwise idyllic childhood inside this house. The mansion had seen better days by the time I was a teenager, and whenever my father and I walked past its graying façade, my father wondered aloud if the house was unoccupied and whether the descendants of the family's patriarch were trying to sell the property. Gene confirmed that the clan had sold the crumbling mansion when he was in his twenties, splitting the proceeds among themselves.

I hadn't known that Gene came from old money when we were younger; our public science high school didn't exactly attract the truly rich. Baguio's wealthy sent their children to Brent, an exclusive private school originally established by the American colonial government to educate white students. Our school had its share of upper-middle-class kids whose doctor and lawyer parents bought them expensive gadgets and clothes, but most of us were middle- and lower-middle-class children who attended the school because our parents believed its rigorous curriculum would eventually buy us the social privilege of studying at a top Filipino university. Gene hadn't been particularly flashy about his wealth, or former wealth, though I do remember that he never forgot to include his middle name on his quizzes, and that our teachers, whose memories of Baguio's history reached farther back than mine, never skipped over his middle name during roll call.

Gene's childhood home came to house a hotel, a restaurant, and even a bank for government employees, and these days, a metal sign bearing a new name for the building that vaguely alludes to its storied past obscures the arched pediment bearing the family's initial. Gene's family had relinquished ownership of the mansion to those who sought to profit from its storied grandness, and so it was easy for me to forget how difficult it was for them to renounce the prestige of their name. Gene was a proud member of their family, though his easygoing nature oftentimes allowed me to forget that he came from old money. When I took a cab from the house my taxi-driver grandfather had built more than half a century ago to Gene's house in the outer suburbs, I hadn't yet fully grasped how his family had clung to the power of their name, despite no longer calling home the mansion that once represented its prestige.

* * *

Gene's house in the suburbs was a simple one-story affair. A group of young people were setting up a tent in the front yard when I arrived. A young woman answered the door, and let me inside when I said I had come to visit Gene. A group of middle-aged men and women were seated around a large dining table at the far end of the hall, and they raised their heads to look at me as the young woman explained I was just a friend of Gene's. I smiled at them as I sank into a living room couch, while they quickly lost interest in me. They turned back to each other, continuing a conversation I had interrupted with my arrival.

Gene emerged from their inner hallway, red-eyed and distraught. I rose from my seat as soon as he saw me, and he spread his arms and pulled me into a tight embrace. "Thank you for coming," he said, loosening his grip. As we took our seats, I told myself that visiting him was a good idea, despite having come unaccompanied, with only Gene to ease my introduction into the tense and private space of a grieving home.

I could sense a loosening in Gene as he talked about how it had been so sudden, how it was too easy to believe that his mother was only resting in her bedroom, even if her body lay in a casket at the other end of the living room. "But I guess I have to accept it, if God willed this," he said, staring into space. "I have to be strong for my niece." I was taken aback by Gene's resolve. I struggled to accept my father's passing a year on.

We talked about how we were coping, and how, for both of us, the suddenness made our loss more difficult to process. Soon, we were joking around and gossiping about our friends from high school. He was laughing, as was I, and for a few moments it was easy to forget we were at a wake. Our grief made us vulnerable, allowing us to be particularly receptive to the joys of the moment as well as its sadness, and we laughed even as we talked about the parents we missed, about how frightening it was to adjust to a world in which his mother and my father had ceased to exist.

A middle-aged woman approached us, and Gene introduced her as his aunt. He excused himself when he was called outside to help set up the tent in their yard. Left alone with his aunt, who had settled in the chair facing me, I asked her if Gene's mother was her sister. "She's my sister," she confirmed to me, and I looked her straight in the eye as I said, "I'm sorry." She gave a resigned, nonchalant shrug as her eyes darted toward the casket beside the door, and she said, with a sigh, "Well."

The young woman who had answered the door entered the living room and poured a bag of mints into a candy bowl before Gene's aunt took her hand and pulled her toward her. "This is my daughter," his aunt said, stroking the young woman's shoulder. I smiled at the young woman, who seemed not to see me as her eyes scanned the room. "She went to City High, just like you and Gene, but she went to the arts section instead of the science section. But now she's into the sciences," she said, smiling at her daughter, who continued to look away from us. She didn't appear to be anxious or fidgety: she leaned into her mother's embrace as she crossed her legs and raised her chin, avoiding my eye with a practiced ease.

"That's so interesting," I said, trying to be polite and reassuring, in case the daughter was nervous or shy. She continued to fix her eyes above my head.

"I came to comfort Gene because I've just lost my father, so I know how it feels," I said.

"Oh, so you know." The older woman smiled.

She asked me what I did for a living, and so I told her that I was a writer and had recently earned my PhD in New Zealand. "You're so young, and you have a PhD?" she asked, sounding genuinely awed. Her daughter, who was still seated beside her, continued to look away. "What did you do your PhD in?" Gene's aunt asked.

I told her that it was in creative writing. She asked me if I was going to go back to New Zealand, and I replied that it wasn't the best country to be a writer—though they had given me a scholarship to do a PhD, I said, it was a small economy with few jobs.

"Excuse me, excuse me," she said, cutting me off by waving her hand. "Writers aren't in demand anywhere. It's like getting a degree in political science. What are you going to do with a degree like that?" she asked, with a smugness that challenged any questioning.

"You could work in a think tank," I said, as a knee-jerk response. I felt the need to defend myself, and so I said, "In my case, I'm getting a lot of freelance work. I was recently paid by a news company in Australia to write a series of articles."

"But you can't live in Australia on what you make writing those articles, right?" she said, with an amused smile. "You couldn't possibly support yourself in Australia on that income, which is why you're here."

"I'm doing it to build my portfolio," I said, confused by the turn the conversation had taken. I didn't expect Gene's aunt to lavish me with gratitude for coming to her sister's wake, but neither did I expect her to make subtle jabs at my career choices as I comforted her grieving nephew and offered her my condolences.

In the course of our exchange, which was by turns friendly and strangely acrimonious, I mentioned that I had lived in America, explaining, when she asked if I had been there for work, that I had attended graduate school there. Perhaps in a misguided attempt to resist her subtle belittlements, I noted that I had earned an MFA from one of the top creative writing programs in the country and that it was considered a terminal degree, adding that I had only done a PhD in New Zealand so that I could have more time to write. She interrupted me again by saying, "So let me get this straight, you did a PhD in New Zealand because they wouldn't recognize your MFA?"

She narrowed her eyes as she said this, assessing the details shared about my life with her private, distorted logic. I glanced at her daughter, who seemed as though she preferred to let her mother take care of this exchange entirely.

"They did recognize my MFA. You don't do a PhD in creative writing in the hopes of getting a job in New Zealand. Even my Kiwi classmates weren't attending the program to raise their job prospects," I protested, feeling increasingly self-conscious.

The other guests glanced toward me, without really looking at me: their eyes skimmed over the top of my head, and when I returned their evasive glances with a polite smile, their eyes would flick away, as though they hadn't seen me at all. And yet I remained rooted to my seat, baffled by this woman's rudeness, trying to convince myself that the strange conversation I'd found myself in would make sense to me as I flailed in my attempts to understand it.

* * *

I felt a lingering sense of unease when I returned home. It was frustrating to acknowledge how Gene's aunt had gotten under my skin, confidently deploying her willful ignorance to humiliate me. She'd dispensed her insults effortlessly, without once losing her poise.

I messaged Roy, a mutual friend from high school, who had told me that he wanted to go to the wake but couldn't figure out the logistics of attending. I told him that I had just returned home from Gene's, and that Gene seemed glad I came. "He's hurting, but I think he'll be okay," I said, and Roy agreed. Then I added, "It felt weird in their house. Almost no one wanted to look at me."

"I'm not surprised, knowing his family," Roy replied. "Only Gene and his siblings are nice. His relatives, though? I can't stand them."

I told him that Gene's aunt was particularly awful. "That's why I didn't want to go there alone," Roy replied. "I was waiting for Ben to accompany me."

I had held on to the foolhardy belief that Gene's relatives would be as generous and open as Gene, deceiving myself into thinking that our grief would momentarily ease the invisible barriers that separated us. It seemed that only Gene and I had reached across this barrier to find solace in our shared grief.

* * *

I stood to leave when Gene returned. As Gene thanked me for coming, his aunt also stood and asked for my name. "It's Monica," I said, obliging her. She then asked me for my last name, which I haltingly gave her, wondering why she needed to know. She appeared startled and asked me if I was related to the former chancellor of UP Baguio.

"That's my mom," I said, hesitating. Her face lit up with recognition. "No wonder the name sounds familiar!" she exclaimed. Her face softened, and it took some time for me to understand what this meant.

Nothing I had achieved on my own, apparently, earned me her respect, but maybe, if she had known earlier that my mother had once occupied a position of power, I wouldn't have had to put up with her insults. It amused me to think that she'd confer so much respect to my family name when, in 2006, our city's elite had vehemently opposed my mother's reelection as chancellor of UP Baguio, choosing instead to support a local ophthalmologist who had no experience in academia. My mother won the race, but it sticks in my memory how our city's elite believed, despite my mother's credentials, that she was unqualified for the position she held, for no reason apart from the fact that she wasn't one of them.

I paid my respects to Gene's mother, whose peaceful expression behind a pane of glass bore no trace of her previous suffering that Gene had described to me. I regretted that this was our first introduction; I would have liked to meet the woman who raised Gene to be the man he is.

"Tito's going to sing for us later," Gene's cousin announced, and a large man standing near the dining table bowed as people clapped. I clapped out of politeness. When I said goodbye to the group, even the family singer looked away, as though I had never set foot in their house at all.

Outside, Gene gave me another hug before we parted. "Let's keep in touch," he said. It seemed I had done the right thing in visiting him, though it was time for us to go our separate ways.

James

Light flickers between the leaves and tendrils of your foster mother's backyard garden. Two figures emerge from the dusk of memory. You are the white, dark-eyed, restless teenager, chasing the smaller, dark-haired, brown-skinned child.

The dining room lamp is switched on. Dinner is about to be served, and your foster mother and my parents are waiting. But we don't head indoors, not yet. We prefer to stay outside, chasing each other until the darkness snatches our figures away from each other's sight.

Despite your rough-and-tumble way of playing tag, you never chase me into your foster mother's unruly garden. "There are snakes in there," you tell me, perhaps repeating what she told you (but without her heavy French accent). I don't need to be warned. My fear of the dark is enough to keep me away.

When night falls, we return to your house, where your foster mother gives you a stern look before telling you to set the table. She complains about your slowness. Your name rings in the air as brightly as the lamp that hangs, like a golden, basketed fruit, over the table.

"Ja-mes, your hands are dirty."

"Ja-mes, go get the ice cream."

You narrow your eyes and fall silent.

You retreat to your room after dinner. She speaks to my parents of the liquor that fed you in the womb, of your slowness at school, of your rock-hard stubbornness that only cracks open to reveal your rage.

You laugh your heart out the next time we visit you. Your fingers dance under my armpits, and your name rings in my throat when I scream in protest.

On our next visit, you are gone from that house filled with musty, doily-covered furniture. That house covered in vines that are never trimmed. We listen to your voice as it bodies forth from a telephone receiver, from a state school in the big city.

Your foster mother winces as she holds the phone to her ear, and I can see how your words sting. But your voice turns gentle when the receiver is handed to me. Your words float out from the static, and I cling to them, wondering whether even your breath will be muted, snatched away.

My family has since returned to our country. But years after my parents receive your foster mother's final letter to them, I return to America. Unable to find you, I imagine you a grown man, walking down a darkening city street, your eyes turned down, never speaking, never making these scenes in my mind seem real.

What feels more real is your impish grin and your dark eyes laughing, brightening the room of memory, the same way in which that dinner lamp, if someone still switches it on, brightens that lonely, dusty house, faintly illuminating that dark, unkempt garden, reaching into the hollows of those bushes, until the eyes of snakes, touched by the light, begin to shine.

Thirty Minutes and a World Apart

The day before Typhoon Mangkhut made landfall in the Philippines, we had every reason to panic and every reason to remain calm. It was supposed to be the strongest typhoon in the world in 2018, and was only slightly weaker than Typhoon Haiyan, which had devastated the city of Tacloban in 2013. The typhoon was reported to be bigger than the entire island of Luzon, and Baguio wouldn't be far from its center as it tore through the island. I sought comfort in my memories of past storms, telling myself that we had previously survived the floods and power outages left in their wake. In a nation like the Philippines, constantly battered by typhoons during the monsoon season, one learns how to live with the dangers that tropical storms bring. And yet as my mother and I followed weather updates, stocked up on food, and braced for the storm, I imagined our roof flying away, and with it, my father's books and handwritten poetry drafts. The physical proof of his existence, to which my mother and I clung as we mourned, would swirl into the sky, swallowed up by its angry churning.

We were better placed to weather Mangkhut than many others. My mother's father, Lolo Andoy, an immigrant from the northern plains of the Ilocos region, selected the location where our house now stands at a time when ample land was available to those who came to the mountain town from nearby lowland provinces, seeking work and a fresh start. He chose a plot near the city center, in the middle of a flat patch of land that has proved, over the years, to be a safe spot during typhoon season, since the land is stable, far from the city's many slopes that are prone to landslides.

The house my grandfather built kept us safe when Typhoon Mang-khut made landfall in the early hours of September 15, 2018. At around two in the morning, I awoke to the sound of wind whistling and objects crashing outside. There was a loud bang in our house—a living room window had been blown open, and my mother rushed from her bedroom to close it. The wind howled, and we slept fitfully.

The next day, we waited for the storm to ease; though we were afraid, we knew, somehow, that we were safe. When power returned that evening, we charged our phones and reassured everyone who had messaged us. Cut off from the world for a few hours, we had no idea of the extent of Typhoon Mangkhut's destruction, while our alarmed relatives and friends from around the world had seen the videos and heard the news.

As we scanned our social media feeds, it became clear that some-thing terrible had happened near our city. An entire mountainside had collapsed on a village. Almost a hundred people feared dead. It had happened in the next town, in a village called Ucab.

My mother and I looked at each other in disbelief. It was *that* Ucab, whose name had once been a joke in our family, simply because no one among us knew where it was.

* * *

I was in high school when I first learned to take a jeep by myself to the city center. At thirteen years old, I was taking baby steps into adulthood, and my parents would accompany me to the jeepney stop near our house and wait until I was safely ensconced in a jeep and headed to my high school. The jeeps I took bore signs like "Plaza-Liteng-Pacdal" or "Plaza-Navy Base"—indicating the city center and familiar neighborhoods—painted on their sides.

Every once in a while, I'd see a jeepney with the sign "Plaza-Ucab" painted on its side. Unlike the other jeeps headed to town, which were cheery and shiny with tassels that waved at us from the thin poles rising from the vehicle's headlights, the Ucab jeeps were drab, lacking ornamentation, and marked by traces of dust, sometimes even caked mud, on their tires and sides. They were always full, and their passengers oftentimes bore the features of the Indigenous groups of the Cordillera. Once in a while, we'd see young men holding on to the bars of the jeep's back door, where they stood, the straps of their Indigenous Sagada-weave backpacks flapping in the wind. Though Baguio is the biggest city in the Cordillera Region, the Indigenous peoples of the Cordillera, collectively referred to as "Igorots" (though belonging to different, distinct ethnic groups), are a minority in the city. The sight of the jeeps full of Igorots from a faraway neighborhood called Ucab gave me, as a teenager, the feeling that I'd encountered something foreign and strange.

Some of the passengers from Ucab would disembark near the gates of my high school, and before flag ceremony you'd see them grouped together, dressed in flared cowboy jeans and cowboy shirts. Sometimes one of them would show off a pair of newly bought cowboy boots to his friends, who'd rib him in a heavily accented Ilocano. My classmates from our high school's elite science class and I listened to Eminem and Britney Spears and would never be caught dead listening to country music. We would stare at the Indigenous students from a distance, mortified, wondering how they could take such pride in being so uncool.

After I had waved down the Ucab jeep by mistake several times, thinking it was a "regular" jeep like the ones coming from Pacdal or Navy Base, my mother started teasing me about putting me on the Ucab jeep. I bristled at her joke; the Ucab jeeps were always full, and what would the Igorots think if I tried to use the jeep that was obviously meant for them? Like many children of Baguio, I grew up hearing Igorot jokes from classmates and elderly relatives, steeped in the kind of deep-seated prejudice that takes years of conscious unlearning to undo.

When my curiosity got the better of me, I asked friends from school where Ucab was. They stared at me blankly, as though I had asked them to locate a faraway galaxy. Relatives and friends of my parents also gave me puzzled looks when asked. They had seen the jeeps, and we all knew the village was nearby, but no one could tell me exactly where it was. It didn't help that none of my classmates and none of my parents' friends were from there, or knew anyone from there.

* * *

Ucab, as I learned after the disaster, is just a thirty-minute jeepney ride from Baguio and is a village in Itogon, a town southeast of Baguio. It's one of many villages that sprang up around the mines established by the Americans during their colonization of the Philippines in the early twentieth century. Baguio's development during the early to mid-twentieth century was fueled by gold, extracted from the mountains in small encampments surrounding the city. These mining communities were increasingly forgotten as the city grew and forgot about its roots, especially as it became a popular tourist destination for lowland Filipinos attracted to its cooler temperatures, pine forest parks, golf courses, and American colonial houses.

When the big mining corporations operating in the province of Benguet scaled back their operations in the 1980s, Baguio became further removed from the mining villages at its outskirts. There were jobs aplenty in the city, and its inhabitants, many of them lowland Filipinos like my grandfather and his descendants, didn't seek work in the mining villages. Instead, the hinterlands of the Cordilleras became a steady source of workers for the mines, which had been taken over by small-scale independent operators when the big mining corporations left.

The two buildings in Ucab buried beneath the collapsed mountainside were bunkhouses owned by Benguet Corporation, a privately owned mining company, near an old mining tunnel also owned by the company. Although Benguet Corporation has officially ceased operations in Ucab, it grants independent contractors access to its abandoned tunnel and bunkhouses, who in turn employ miners of their own. Most of these miners are Indigenous men hailing from neighboring provinces such as Mountain Province, Abra, and Ifugao.

According to Leonida Tundagui, an independent researcher I spoke to on Facebook who interviewed miners employed in the area during relief operations following the disaster, the Benguet Corporation collects 40 percent of all revenue from gold extracted from its abandoned mines. Independent contractors collect a 20 percent cut, leaving the remaining 40 percent for the miners to divide among themselves. This arrangement allows Benguet to collect money from rent and profits without shouldering the responsibility of maintaining the tunnels or providing safety equipment for the miners.

It is a system as rife with exploitation as it is dangerous; many miners have died of asphyxiation and gas poisoning in "abandoned" tunnels. Since these miners aren't official employees of Benguet, the company isn't liable when accidents, or even deaths, occur. The miners are basically on their own when they risk their lives underground.

Many of those who died in the landslide were from the village of Cababuyan, in the town of Hingyon, in the province of Ifugao. According to Ermie Bahatan, a social worker with roots in Cababuyan whose Facebook post led to our acquaintance, men from Ifugao work in the mines to support their families during the fallow period of rice production. Employment opportunities in Ifugao are often limited to low-paying farm work, and although government construction projects offer some job openings while locals wait for the harvest season, many don't possess the necessary skills to apply. The mines, then, become an attractive, if risky, option.

Upon their return to Cababuyan, the men, Ermie says, describe work in the mines as difficult and often treacherous. They count themselves lucky if the contractors supply them with equipment and safety gear such as boots, head caps, flashlights, and hammers. Life is tough in Ucab, but with families to feed and few opportunities at home, they have little choice but to see their contracts through.

Local authorities now say that the inhabitants of the affected part of Ucab were told to evacuate days before Typhoon Mangkhut made landfall, as a crack had been spotted in the mountaintop overlooking the settlement. Baguio and its environs had experienced a month of endless rain ahead of the storm, and so the soil of the mountains surrounding Ucab was already soft when Mangkhut swept across Luzon. It was a dangerous situation, but many had traveled all the way from Ifugao, seven hours away. With no relatives nearby with whom they could sit out the storm, there was nowhere they could evacuate to except for the bunkhouses where they took shelter on that fateful afternoon.

These men were used to placing their lives at risk in the mines every day, and I can imagine how staying put during the storm, for them, was not much different from the everyday risks they took when they went underground. They knew the area, had been inside the mountains themselves—who could say whether the police officers who knocked on their doors to warn them knew better about the dangers of the area? Who could say which mountain would collapse, when all of them were riddled with holes and saturated with rain? Staying put during a storm, perhaps, was another gamble the workers were willing to take. As usual, with some luck and a prayer, they'd survive.

* * *

When I first thought of writing this essay, I talked to two of my friends, both Indigenous women, who knew people who had gone to Ucab to report on rescue operations or to provide relief. While we spoke, they realized that they, too, hadn't known where Ucab was until the day after the storm. One of them, a doctor, had patients from Ucab, and had a vague awareness of its being in the nearby town of Itogon but never really knew where Ucab actually was until after the landslide. My other friend had seen the Ucab jeeps, but kept confusing the village with Lucnab, a neighborhood within Baguio's city limits.

When I was in high school, I once boarded an Ucab jeep by mistake—it was a strange accident, involving, if I remember right, a driver who stopped when I waved his vehicle down, who also refused to start the jeep again when I had entered and was looking for a vacant seat. He probably realized he had made a mistake—the passengers of the jeep, country folk in simple dresses, denim jackets, and cuffed jeans, some with large bundles at their feet, simply shook their heads when I looked at them. When I think about the incident now, I realize that I was intruding on their space, unable to see the invisible circle of kinship to which I did not belong.

* * *

Right after the tragedy, the Department of Environment and Natural Resources issued an order to cease small-scale mining in the Cordillera Region. In response, those living in or near Ucab complained that without mining, they would not survive. Some have admitted on television that as soon as the dust settles, they'll return to the mines. In response, presidential spokesperson Harry Roque suggested vegetable farming as an alternative means of livelihood for these miners. Though vegetable farming is one of Benguet's premier industries, revenues for farmers are dismal as middlemen buy their vegetables at rock-bottom prices. Farmers also shoulder transportation costs for their vegetables on top of costs incurred for fertilizer and pesticides, which cuts into their earnings significantly. Many farmers accrue debts to cover these costs, and suicide rates in the community are alarmingly high. In the Cordilleras, mining is seen as a more lucrative line of work than vegetable farming, despite the risks involved.

A miner on TV said, when asked about vegetable farming, "Where are you going to plant vegetables here, when all of this is stony ground?"

* * *

Almost a week after the landslide, I met Ester Fianza, a retired professor at Benguet State University who was born and raised in Itogon's población and was familiar with the area. She had promised to take me to Ucab, and we met that morning at a Jollibee in the center of the city, near the midtown street where jeeps headed for Ucab, and other mining villages in Benguet's interior, departed from the city. Over burgers and peach mango pie, we talked about how small-scale mining in Itogon had turned the mountains surrounding these villages into blocks of Swiss cheese. "Each company of miners has to pull two or three hundred sacks of Nava stones from those tunnels per week, from which they extract gold. You can just imagine how many stones they extract from those tunnels in a year, or in a decade," Ester said, in between sips of hot chocolate. "It's not like they can return the stone to the tunnels. There's nothing left in those mountains. It's just hollow ground."

According to Ester, most of those who live in Ucab, and many other mining villages surrounding our city, aren't originally from this part of Benguet. Many escaped poverty in the Cordilleran hinterlands, lured to Itogon with the promise of good money in the mines. "You'll have a hard time persuading them to abandon mining," she added. She told me about how, after receiving their cut from the group's earnings, many of the miners take the Ucab jeep to Baguio, where they head for the bars. True enough, Magsaysay Avenue, the street we were on, is the last stop for jeeps coming into the city from the mining villages and is known for its honky-tonk bars. There was a slight whiff of judgment in her voice as she talked about how these men wasted their precious earnings on drinks and women, but she agreed with me when I pointed out that their work was difficult and dangerous and they likely needed some respite from the drudgery of the mines. I learned later that her father had died young and that her mother had fed and sent her children to school by operating a small sari-sari store. To Ester, perhaps, these miners who splurged their hard-earned cash seemed disastrously unwise.

Later, as we sat in the jeep to Ucab, a pair of elderly ladies wearing colorful Sagada-weave jackets stared at me as I spoke to Ester in a smattering of Tagalog and English. I cannot speak Ilocano, the de facto lingua franca of the Igorot tribes, and I probably stuck out in the jeep like a sore thumb as Ester told me about her hometown, the Itogon población, and about how their public pool was washed out by Typhoon Mangkhut. "Is this your first time leaving the city to see Benguet?" she asked me, with a smile. Perhaps it was obvious to the others on the jeep, as they gave me strange looks, that I was there to see the landslide. I wondered if my presence was entirely welcome.

It helped that Ester was there with me, since she served to ease my welcome into this circle of strangers, who answered my questions in Ilocano when I said them aloud in Tagalog—she was there, anyway, to translate. The teenagers fiddled with their phones, and the young men, I noticed, now eschewed cowboy fashion for hip-hop clothing. As we left the central city, a man in cuffed jeans and worn leather jacket, Sagada-weave bag slung onto his back, grabbed on to the bars of the jeep's door and clung to them, standing at the jeep's entrance for the entire trip.

It's beautiful outside the city: the mountains remain covered in pine trees and native bush, and they rise and fall like waves, fading to light green and blue in the distance. Ester pointed at the mountains that big mining companies had once tunneled into in search of gold, reminding me that these mountains, rendered unstable by decades of mining, could also kill.

Small landslides began to dot the mountainsides, and the road grew narrower and dustier as we approached Ucab. A portion of the road leading into the village had just collapsed, and our driver squeezed the jeep into what was left of it as a policeman directed traffic. "A German engineer once told us that it would only take one big storm or earthquake for this village to be swept downhill," Ester said, as we entered the village center. "Underneath? It's all riddled with holes."

We disembarked from the jeep and walked down Ucab's narrow, dusty main street, stepping on dry patches of red spittle stains, chewed betel nut remains spat out on the road. I spotted more than one church, and signs hanging from windows and doorframes proclaiming "God is good" and "Jesus saves." I noticed a little boy wearing a T-shirt that read, "God is awesome." Even before my visit, I had been taken aback by the fervent religiosity of these people I had seen in televised reports, who had lost friends and loved ones in the landslide: when interviewed, they all said that although it hurt to lose a loved one, it was all part of God's plan.

As we walked farther down the street, we saw a water delivery truck filling a metal tank attached to a house. I noticed that almost all of the houses, whether made of unfinished concrete blocks or tin, had water tanks connected to them. Ester told me that Ucab, like much of Itogon, was not serviced by the local water district, and that households in the village needed water delivered from private companies in Baguio.

We were far away from the wreckage at the bottom of the mountain, but when we reached a certain spot on the street, the unmistakable smell of decaying bodies hit us like a wave. We found a spot where we could get a good view of the landslide, and stepped onto a concrete platform by the side of the road where onlookers had gathered. My stomach lurched as my gaze moved downward, toward the bottom of the ravine. Ester beckoned me to stand beside her.

The landslide was bigger than I had imagined when I saw it in pictures and on my TV screen: an entire mountainside was practically gone. Orange tents had been erected on a hill below us, with a whiteboard bearing the names of those still missing. Farther downhill, policemen in blue shirts and miners wearing hardhats and the orange uniform of the Philex Mining Corporation congregated beneath another tent. Both groups, I'd been told, had volunteered to retrieve bodies from the rubble and to rescue survivors, if they found any.

The landslide had headed straight for the two bunkhouses, missing other houses in its path. One bunkhouse had been full of miners and their families who had evacuated their homes at the height of the storm, thinking that the bunkhouse, often used as an evacuation area during storms, was the safest place to take shelter. The other bunkhouse was a converted chapel, where families and young musicians had gathered to practice for the next day's mass.

Reading the news, I imagined the bunkhouses to be at the foot of the mountain, and wondered why people believed they'd be a safe refuge. But the bunkhouses hadn't actually been on the mountainside at all, and a villager pointed out to us that they were some distance away. Indeed, the landslide somehow missed houses in its path, some of which still clung precariously to the mountainside, and instead found the bunkhouses that appeared, from where I stood, to be nearly a kilometer away from the foot of the mountain. According to a villager who emerged from the barangay hall to speak to us, there had been another, smaller landslide near the bunkhouses, and these two landslides met at the very place where these people thought they'd be kept safe.

Two helicopters emerged from behind the mountaintops of the next village, filling the air with their threatening hum.

"Looks like they found someone," Ester said, pointing at a man below us. It took me some time to find him, but there he was, frantically waving a white handkerchief.

* * *

It started drizzling, and we decided to head back to the city. We boarded the same jeep we took into Ucab, and across from us sat a woman who smiled before introducing herself as a member of one of the original families of Ucab. She told Ester that near her house, another old mining tunnel had collapsed, and so Ester told her the same story about the German engineer who said it wouldn't take much for Ucab's main center to slide down into the ravine. The woman smiled, as though to be polite, just as two men in worn, cuffed jeans grabbed onto the railings of the jeep's entrance, planting their mud-caked sandals onto the platforms flanking the door. There they clung, as the jeep made its steady climb up the winding highway, past achingly beautiful scenery and bald spots left by landslides. They held on until we reached the city limits and some passengers disembarked, upon which they clambered inside and found seats.

* * *

The evening before I visited Ucab with Ester, Ermie texted me, say-ing she'd be at the disaster site the next day to accompany people from Cababuyan as they waited for the remains of their relatives to be recovered from the rubble. The Ifugao believe that their dead must be buried near their ancestors, or else their spirits will hound their fami-lies, forever restless until their remains have been brought home. This made me think of my own father, who was buried in Baguio, far away from his hometown of Zamboanga. Even if he had made Baguio his home since the early 1980s, his stories always drifted back to the city of his childhood, where the food was always better, the people more welcoming, the festivals grander than anything I had ever seen in Baguio. Memory, like the spirit, will always seek its home, even when our bodies carry us to faraway places.

Ermie sent me the photos she had of barrio Cababuyan, pictures of terraced hills planted with rice, mountaintops blanketed in fog, and rice stalks turning golden in the sun, ready for harvesting. I can imagine how the spirits of the dead would want to return to this place: in pictures, it's beautiful and quiet, far away from the violence of a storm and a mountainside burying people alive. Relatives made the seven-hour trip from Ifugao to retrieve the remains of their dead, hoping to give them a proper burial in the land of their birth. Perhaps the dead, who made this journey to work in the mines, found com-fort in knowing that no matter how far they traveled, and no matter how dangerous their work was, their loved ones would find them, eventually, and bring them home.

* * *

My lolo Andoy did not work in the mines, but drove a jeepney, and later on, a taxi. He reaped many of the benefits of a flourishing econ-omy that was fueled by the success of the nearby mines: he came to operate his own fleet of taxis and sent all his daughters to col-lege. The life my parents provided for me in Baguio was comfortable, and thanks to choices my lolo Andoy made early in life, we were far removed from the poverty that would have awaited us if my grandfa-ther hadn't moved his family to the city.

If one is a new immigrant from the barrio with few connections, one's success depends, to a huge extent, on luck. My grandparents worked hard and earned their success, but in many ways they were lucky too: my grandfather chose the right business, met good people, and found a vacant lot in the right part of town when land was still cheap. A better life for their children, when my grandparents moved to Baguio, wasn't guaranteed, but they still grabbed at the chance, taking a necessary leap of faith to lift their family out of poverty. It worked out for them, but others aren't as lucky.

It is easy to forget how the poor have few choices in life when one is removed, by geography and several generations, from poverty. We forget how our ancestors made leaps of faith to break the cycle of intergenerational poverty in our own families. Here in the city, we forget that the same is occurring right now, right at our doorstep: men, sometimes entire families, uprooting themselves from small towns in the Cordilleras to find better work in the mines near Baguio. Considering the few choices they have, it's a gamble they are willing to take, even if it could cost their lives.

Polina

Something didn't seem right when her page landed in my Facebook recommendations. We hadn't spoken in years, and her Facebook name, Diamond Carter, couldn't possibly belong to someone like Polina, whose face was just as Filipino as mine. Whatever stylishness or glamour she sought from such an alias didn't match the way she presented herself in her profile picture: her shoulder-length hair was unfashionably trimmed, the shot's harsh lighting only serving to bring forth a frumpiness that was new to me.

The last time I had heard from Polina was seven years before—she had asked me to give her feedback on a novel manuscript, and I tried to be kind in my suggestions even as I was at a loss for kind things to say. I received no response to my feedback, and I eventually realized that she had blocked me on social media. Her reappearance in my Facebook feed felt like a cosmic joke; seven years hadn't been enough for me to recover from the shock of being cut off by a friend I had spent long, laugh-filled nights with in our college dorm. Was she trying to disguise herself from me by putting on a ridiculous name, even as the same Polina stared at me from my screen, eyes narrowed, lips twisting into a wry smirk?

I tapped on her profile picture to reveal what appeared to be an author page that had more than a thousand followers. She identified herself as the head coach of a writing organization with over twenty thousand followers. This baffled me. Her writing that was available online, which I'd find whenever my confusion over the end of our friendship sent me down a Google rabbit hole, was written in a stilted

English, in a style that seemed willfully amateurish. But people were paying good money for her classes, and it appeared that she was also handing out prizes.

I searched the name of her writing group, and then I found a Facebook page calling her organization a scam.

* * *

It's likely that she had observed me more closely than I had observed her in high school, for she had more memories of watching me from afar. I was only marginally aware of her, since we'd barely crossed paths: I was an underperformer in our public high school's elite science class, while she was a top performer in the school's crowded regular section. She'd startle us back to wakefulness at school programs by singing and delivering speeches, her perkiness becoming the object of sly jokes as we made our way back to our classrooms. My classmates knew that she was outdoing us, that she would go far, farther than any of us, even if she hadn't been smart enough to be admitted into our elite section occupying its separate set of buildings. Though we occasionally complained about their uncouthness and lack of class, we were barely aware of the students in the regular section, and Polina seemed too sprightly and driven to be one of them and not one of us. We weren't too taken aback when she outdid the writers from our science class, me included, to become the school paper's editor-in-chief—not because we admired her writing but because she seemed to be a person who got what she wanted.

Polina occupied the fringes of my consciousness, for I was too busy trying to survive the bullying that came at me in unexpected moments, as I walked down a hill to class or spent recess hunched over a book. From afar, she seemed perky and pleasant, uninvolved in the bullying I suffered at the hands of my classmates. I had no idea at the time that she was observing me, making her own conclusions. In college, she'd admit to me that I had seemed proud and self-absorbed, that she never imagined us becoming friends. I didn't have the courage to reveal to her that I had been afraid of my peers, that I lowered my head and avoided people's eyes out of habit, so as not to offer up the softest parts of myself to those keen on hurting me. In college I strove to leave my past behind, and to admit to anyone, even to her, that I had been bullied in high school meant revealing to people that I, too, could be an object of scorn.

I went to Manila for college, hoping that this would allow me to shake off the constrictions I had once felt in the company of peers who believed that they knew me, just because they had spent years witnessing me assume an identity I was eager to shed. I knew that some of my classmates from high school belonged to the incoming freshman class of the University of the Philippines, and I decided to avoid them if I could. But I didn't know that Polina had also gotten into UP until my roommate and I emerged from our dorm room to meet our neighbors, and a cheerful, bespectacled girl pulled away from her group to call out my name.

The warm exuberance that filled her voice as she reached out her hand was something I'd expect from a friend. I clasped her hand, trying to place her face, and a flood of recognition ran through me as we erupted in happy shrieks. In this strange, humid city, I was ready for anything, and I took the sudden friendship of a girl I had known for some time, though from afar, as a reassuring sign.

She loved writing, Polina told me over dinner in our dorm cafeteria, but she wanted to be a doctor, which was why she was majoring in biology. The year she became editor of our school paper, an essay I wrote won second place in the youth division of the Palanca Awards, the most prestigious literary award in the Philippines—and she knew all about it, she said, smiling and chattering away as though we had known each other forever. I was flattered by her eagerness, for I had no clue that she had paid any attention to me in high school. Back then she'd appeared too busy to take notice of me, her cheery optimism insulating her from the rest of us as she gaily snagged the achievements she was destined to claim. I felt myself warming up to her as she spoke, becoming self-assured when she asked me about my classes and the writing I had done after my Palanca.

I'd see her marching down our corridor in the mornings, the stuffed heads of her Scooby-Doo bedroom slippers bobbing up and down, matching her determined stride. I felt steadied by her friendship, for as I walked down the long, tree-lined avenues of our sprawling campus filled almost entirely with students who'd graduated at the top of their high school class, I found my initial resolve to leave behind my past failures slipping away. With Polina, however, I felt less alone. In her company, I felt my world expanding, like a pair of lungs taking breath, as we sat in her room and talked about our brilliant professors, marveling at how things here seemed so much different from our provincial high school where our teachers never cared about what we thought, instead equating education with rote memorization.

Her face lit up with excitement when I asked her if she wanted to get coffee and cakes at an expensive café near our dorm on our second weekend away from home. When I knocked on her door that Saturday, I saw that like me, she had decided to wear a nice skirt and blouse, and a nice pair of dress shoes. The scant servings at our dorm cafeteria left us ravenous, and my skirt's waistband rubbed against my hipbones as we walked down the block to the Chocolate Kiss Café, where professors, tourists, and even the occasional movie star dined. Inside its low-ceilinged, air-conditioned interior, our waiter guided us to a table and handed us our menus. We gave him our orders and giggled as we settled into our cushioned seats. Playacting adulthood on our parents' dime, we felt suffused with a newfound power in this softly lit restaurant, far away from Baguio. We were taking baby steps toward adult sophistication with every bite of cake and sip of coffee, and though we didn't have enough money to leave a tip for our waiter, we were confident that we would do so the next time we came by. For of course there would be a next time: we were adults now, and fully in charge of our lives.

* * *

Eight years later, as a graduate student sitting in my apartment in America, I found myself scrolling through Polina's Facebook profile, struggling to reconcile the girl I'd known with this woman who advertised her wanderings around Manila to "win souls for Jesus." When she wrote a long post telling women our age to "keep our bodies pure for our future husbands," I criticized the sentiment in a comment she immediately deleted.

I had just returned from America when Polina reached out to me again, and was putting together my paperwork for graduate studies in New Zealand when she emailed me her novel manuscript, ready for printing, and ending with a biography that listed all her writing awards from first grade onward. I struggled to control my laughter as

I waded through Polina's garbled sentences and illogical plot points. I had begrudgingly accepted the task of giving feedback on the manuscript, sensing in my friend's messages a certain falseness as she called me "dear Monica," praised me for my recent achievements, and asked me to look at her novel, upon the request of a man bankrolling its publication, because she knew what an "excellent" writer I was. I knew that I was no longer a part of her world, sensing that she could no longer associate with a person like me because I hadn't yet accepted Jesus and wasn't yet saved.

"Would you please stop?" my father said, after I had read aloud another incoherent passage from her book. When I looked up from my laptop screen, I was startled to see his face pinched with pain.

"This just breaks my heart," my father said, rubbing his chest as he gave me a look of reproach. "I have fond memories of that brilliant girl, and this breaks my heart."

Glancing at her words on my computer screen, I felt my amusement evaporate, leaving in its place a faint trace of grief.

* * *

I couldn't quite tell what Polina felt when we learned from her that she had failed her first exam in introductory math, but I was tempted to think that she was taking it well. As others in our dorm crowded around her, holding up their blue books to compare their failing scores with hers, I comforted myself with the thought that she wasn't alone. The anguish she likely felt that evening occupied a marginal place in my consciousness, for I had my own disappointments to grapple with.

I had received the equivalent of a B for my first paper in a basic English class, because, as my professor was inclined to tell me, "Your English is good and you write well, but it's just, I don't know." She was a dour-faced woman who made it seem as if she had better things to do than teach us the basics of composition at 8:30 in the morning, and she shrugged as she handed me back my paper, her "I don't know" a solid, blank wall. In her lectures she'd insert asides about how English majors weren't very smart, comparing us to the engineering majors in the room who, according to her, faced more challenges in completing their degrees. Her "I don't know" was a fence that rose higher the more I tried to guess what I could do to raise my grades.

I began taking frequent walks around our tree-lined campus, feeling an unusual weight pressing down on me, draping itself over my body whenever I tried to push it off. I'd complain about my English professor to my friends in the dorm, who didn't know how to comfort me, for they couldn't tell who was right in this situation: our professors were all brilliant, and so could it be that my professor saw something in my writing that was not to her liking?

I knew that Polina was attending remedial math sessions held at our dorm, and it was impossible for me to imagine her failing introductory math with the way she was poring over her textbooks and scribbling notes at her desk. She confessed to me that her goal, at that point, was simply not to fail, having accepted that she was no longer going to receive top marks in all her courses. And so why did I take offense when she admitted to me, after I delivered yet another rant about my English professor, that she was excelling in basic English? She showed me the papers she had written, the A minuses scribbled above her name. English was the subject I was supposed to be good at, and I was baffled as I read one of her essays. Had she chanced on a kind professor who rewarded her for her efforts despite her graceless and confused sentences?

* * *

The Facebook page calling her writing organization a scam had only one post, claiming that Polina sold writing awards to those willing to pay for them, and that Polina signed these certificates and plaques with both her real name and her fictitious name, Diamond Carter, assigning two different positions to these two identities. As Polina, she was president of the organization, and as "Diamond Carter," she was its head coach. For a few days I sat with my discovery, trying to reconcile the Polina I knew with the puzzling scheme I'd stumbled upon.

A few months passed before "Diamond Carter" reappeared in my Facebook recommendations. Her smirk taunted me this time, hinting at secrets that weren't for me to know. It almost seemed as if her brazenness were meant for me, inviting me to behold the artifice she had successfully created. A lie could become truth, it seemed, as long as enough people believed it.

I messaged the owners of the page that called her organization a scam, telling them how I was shocked to learn that she was now a writing mentor after having read her work. I ended my message by calling her a fraud, without thinking long and hard about what this made me—was I her enemy now, just because in my view, she had claimed an authority that didn't belong to her?

Whoever was behind this page responded to me immediately, writing about the lies Polina had told and the scams she had conceived to trick young writers into handing over their cash. According to this person, Polina made her organization appear more prestigious than it was by inflating her credentials, and used workbooks that were available for free on the internet for her expensive workshops. There were allegations floating around that she charged exorbitant fees for self-published authors and vanity presses to sell their books at a "Grand Bookfair" that she held in nondescript locations without tables or chairs. Apart from this, she'd pretend to be affiliated with publishers who'd threaten to sue her until she agreed to drop their names from her promotional materials. If anyone broke away from her writing organization and tried to expose her fraudulent practices, she'd unleash a swarm of sock puppet accounts to intimidate and harass the whistleblower and their relatives. Apart from selling awards that she signed with both her real name and an alias, she tried to gain legitimacy for her group by giving awards to big names in the Philippine literary scene, currying favor with those who could grant her their powerful endorsements.

I had thought at first that Polina was merely presenting herself as a more capable writer than she actually was, aspiring for the trappings of power without having any interest in growing as a writer. But this person seemed to be describing someone else, not the Polina I'd known. This wasn't the passionate girl who, in college, was eager to learn everything, bravely assessing every obstacle she faced as though it were a mathematical problem that would eventually yield to her prodding.

"We never knew who Polina really was until you reached out to us," the person behind the Facebook page told me. "She was just this social climber in our community who liked kissing ass with publishers and presidents of other writing groups."

I swore to them that this wasn't the Polina I knew, even as I realized that I, too, didn't know who she was.

* * *

Many of my classmates from high school who had graduated with honors hadn't exactly delivered an impressive performance in our first semester, and I rubbed my newly earned "college scholar" status in their faces whenever I had the chance. I believed it to be an act of defiance, rejoicing in the thought that they were now experiencing the same humiliations they had once forced me to endure.

My experience with my freshman composition instructor seemed to have been an unfortunate accident—my literature professor in my second semester loved my writing and oftentimes called on me to explain ideas and images that confused my classmates. After being told repeatedly in high school that I was ugly, I was shocked, and pleasantly surprised, to learn that I was physically attractive. I experimented with my makeup and clothes, earning compliments from former classmates in high school who softened to me as they witnessed my transformation. Shaking off the wariness I had carried with me throughout high school, I found it easier to make friends. I basked in my newfound popularity as I lay on Polina's bed in the evenings, noticing how she was spending more and more time at her desk in front of her books.

Like many people I knew from high school, Polina hadn't made it onto the dean's list. I felt strangely triumphant in her presence, even as her quiet disappointments filled the awkward pauses in our conversations. She swore that she no longer cared about such things because she was getting a good education; those who cared, she said, were people back home who didn't understand how difficult it was to rise to the top at an institution like this. She'd then give me a sad smile before telling me that I was doing so well and that people in our hometown kept asking her if it were true that they wouldn't recognize me now. They'd never understand why I had flourished in a place like this, she'd say, which only convinced her of how small their world remained.

"They just don't get it," she said, fixing a determined look at her Scooby-Doo-encased feet as she crossed her legs. "We've left them all behind, and they don't even know it."

I remember the moments of silence that would follow these statements, in which Polina's disappointments would seep into the air, giving me pause. I tell myself now that I could have said something to reassure her instead of shaking off the discomfort I felt with a joke or a jab at the people we knew from home. Could I have been a little more sensitive to her pain back then, now that I know what became of it?

Many of our conversations devolved into rants: she called our classmates who were attending the local nursing school "doctor's lackeys" who were preparing for "a life of wiping asses" and disparaged "the mediocrities" who planned to study at our local medical school. Though I initially laughed with approval at her insults, gaining a fleeting sense of superiority over the people she belittled, a worrying vehemence seemed to possess her the more she filled our conversations with her fuming. Her purposeful gait I had observed in the mornings took on an air of irritation, her shoulders squared defensively against a difficult world. Her entire body was primed for battle, even as it quietly nursed its hurts.

And what did I do to comfort her? All I did was invite myself to her room, teasing her about her work ethic as I lay in her bed. "The world won't stop if you take a break," I'd say, annoyed by the way she fixed her eyes on her books, refusing to yield to my wheedling. "Look at me," I'd add. "I'm not studying tonight." My restored sense of self-worth was making me indifferent to the anxieties that colored her face whenever I nudged her to pause her work and join me in conversation.

Her growing resentment for me finally seeped into her words one afternoon. "You were so different back then," she said, as I rested my forearm against the edge of her desk, feeling at home in her tiny corner of this shared room. "We'd be watching you from afar and your head was always bent down, like you wanted nothing to do with any of us," she added, smirking at a distant memory that did not belong to this room or to our present life. She chuckled to herself, then spat out the word: "Outcast."

* * *

In the wake of my discoveries online, perhaps I felt the urge to hurt Polina, if only to test the limits of her power. I had known the person who lurked behind this digital façade, and so maybe I wanted to make sure that my old friend was still there, that she continued to nurse a private hurt. It was her pain that made her human all those years ago, for it revealed a part of her that was as lost and confused as I had been. I recoiled at this new version of her that had hardened, hiding away the soft, vulnerable parts of herself from a world on which she chose to inflict her rage.

Or maybe I am simply excusing myself for the cruelty of exposing her on social media—in the end, it was an impulsive act, borne out of my own rage and confusion. I had no right to feel betrayed—her life was now separate from mine, and her schemes had nothing to do with me. If she had betrayed anything, it was merely the past we shared, a friendship that no longer existed. Maybe it was this simple truth that I struggled to accept.

Rina, one of my few friends from high school, saw my Facebook post about Polina and sent me links to business pages Polina had invited her to like. The words "welcome to my team of global champions" snaked across a cover photo, beneath a photograph of a thinner, beaming Polina that had likely been taken when we were in college. On this page, she claimed to "help people from all walks of life achieve growth and success in all areas of life" by guiding them in building a digital business that generated money "even as they slept." It was the kind of smarmy, misleading language I associated with MLMs and pyramid schemes, and I was immediately suspicious.

"It's like she started her own cult," Rina said, as I scrolled down the page.

* This business runs 24/7 even if I am asleep or at work, and even while I'm taking care of my child. I AM NOT KIDDING. THIS IS SO TRUE!

* NO selling, no inventory, no sales quota, no deadlines, no overtime, and we don't have to push anyone to enter the business. This part . . . THIS DEFINITELY GOT MY EYES GLUED ON THIS BUSINESS.

* So if you happen to be like me and you have big dreams for yourself and your loved ones, then DON'T WAIT.

"So that's why she self-plugs like crazy," another friend said, sending me a screenshot of Polina's personal page. Carrying the name "Polly Lacsamana," it was different from the profile page Rina sent me, which also advertised the same "boss-free life" but as "Polina Marie Lacsamana." Another friend sent me a screenshot of a profile bearing the name "Diamond Carter" with a photo of Polina from long ago, which was different from the one featured on the Diamond Carter author page I had first seen. I searched her name on Facebook and found a few more profiles, each with different variations on her name. I asked the owners of the page exposing her writing organization if they knew about this, to which they responded, "She used to have more, but they were taken down after we reported them."

Were these versions of Polina poor copies of the person I once knew, or was I just having trouble recognizing the person she had become?

* * *

In the best of times, our unspoken rivalry could evaporate just as easily as our stories and laughter came to fill its place. When our dorm emptied out on weekends (as most of our dormmates chose to spend this time with relatives living in Manila), I'd come to Polina's room where she'd set aside her books and offer me a packaged Lotte Choco Pie. We'd talk about the cheesy movies and TV shows we'd secretly adored in high school and described to each other our memories of Baguio, which for all its small-mindedness, was the one place that truly felt like home. I missed my father's cooking and his jokes while Polina missed the grandparents who had raised her, especially her grandmother, who had recently passed away. She thought of her grandmother all the time, she said, and talked to her whenever she had the chance to visit her grave. I thought of how my own love for my parents endured across the distances, which felt vast for an only child like me living away from home for the first time. I couldn't imagine losing them, but as Polina spoke about the ways she sought to honor her grandmother's life, I wondered if love alone would sustain me when it was my turn to experience this kind of grief.

Though she was born in Manila where her parents and six siblings still lived, Polina had suffered from breathing problems as a baby, which made her parents decide to leave her with her grandparents in Baguio, where the air was cleaner. Though I found it strange that a young couple would leave their daughter with her grandparents and never return for her, it seemed to have worked out in the end. Her grandfather was a retired judge who, according to Polina, instilled in her a keen sense of right and wrong, as well as a passion for good grammar and the English language. My father had met him a few years before, when Polina and I took a fancy Manila science high school's entrance exam—he had been charmed by the man's ebullience and could see how Polina, whom my father met shortly after, took after him.

She once showed me a story she had written for a creative writing class, and I saw in her work a talent for imagery that would have shone brighter if her sentences were more precise and controlled. Though I was happy that she had found a teacher who delighted in her numerous flights of fancy, I wasn't quite sure if her teacher's unqualified praise was helping Polina develop the kind of discipline that would allow her talent to radiate through. But Polina swore that she had no intentions of becoming a professional writer, and I was happy that she had found some validation in the midst of her many disappointments. Who was I to say that what she was capable of when she continued to astound me with her work ethic?

Her gift for storytelling was undeniable, and I found a balm for my loneliness in the stories she told me about her childhood and the family she adored. She doted on her siblings, whom she did not grow up with but who visited her with their parents whenever they had the chance. But it was her grandparents whom she truly adored and who featured prominently in her stories about being a cherished, pampered child who excelled at school and found happiness in the written word.

"Did I ever tell you that they took me to Europe when I was four years old?" she asked me one day, eyes sparkling with excitement. She described how she had offered up a toast with a little glass to a kind stranger when they dined at a Parisian café, and how they had crossed the Swiss Alps in a train and gazed at ancient, ornate buildings in the great cities they had visited. I was unsure if my mother's promise to take me to Europe would bear actual fruit, and so Polina's story about this vividly remembered trip captivated me. She was a lucky girl, I exclaimed as we sat in my dorm room with its peeling paint and cracks in the walls. Joy rippled across her face when I said this, maybe because—and this has only occurred to me lately—she had succeeded in weaving a tale that beguiled me.

Perhaps I am being cruel in doubting what was likely a joyful event in her early life, accusing her of more than what she is actually guilty of. Perhaps the trip to Europe really happened, and her doting grandparents had wanted to take her along instead of leaving her with her parents in Manila, where she suffered from breathing problems I assumed she'd outgrown by the time we entered college in Manila. Maybe it happened, and yet when I connect it to the many other things I now know about Polina, I'm not sure if I trust her story like I did all those years ago.

Her family came to see her at our university campus every Sunday afternoon, giving her a tiny allowance that was a fraction of what I received from my parents. Unlike most of our dormmates with relatives in Manila, Polina did not spend her weekends at her family's home, instead waiting in our empty dorm for a text from her parents. It occurs to me now that her parents likely struggled to support their seven children, which was why they sent Polina to live with her grandparents. Her childhood trip to Europe may have happened, but did she cling to this memory to make sense of an abandonment that was difficult to comprehend? Time and distance allow me to make such conjectures, for I too was taken by the way she wove together these puzzling threads to create a story that enchanted us both.

* * *

Hi everyone! You can call me Polly. I am a writer, a mom, and a dreamer. Here's my story on how I took the leap of faith to become a digital mompreneur in only two months. I have always dreamed of a bigger and better life for me and my family.

I clicked on the link accompanying this Facebook post, finding myself on a webpage that looked similar to phishing emails I'd occasionally open in my inbox's spam folder, outlining a business opportunity with bold declarations that were intentionally vague. Beneath such vague promises were fake-looking testimonials, featuring smiling couples pictured at the beach or in posh-looking restaurants.

Ben and Theresa, Flagstaff, USA. My husband and I liter-
ally lived in a bad area of Cleveland OH! This business has
allowed us both to quit our horrible corporate jobs and move
across the country—finally enjoying our days together in the
sunshine of Arizona!

This was my friend, who had worked so much harder than I did
in college, who wrote in our high school yearbook that she wanted to
become "a topnotch medical researcher," who had changed her plans
of going to medical school when her biology professors began to com-
mend her abilities as a researcher, conferring on her the best thesis
award in her graduating class. My friend, whose ambition was once
irrepressible, was now asking me for my name and email address so
that I could learn more about a business that "made money for her
while she slept" and "allowed her to spend more time with her child."
Her aspirations in college went far beyond motherhood, and I stared
at the page in disbelief, for I hadn't been around to witness whatever
had loosened her grip on the dreams she once held, replacing them
with this cheap facsimile.

She had included on her webpage an old picture, and from the past
she flashed me the bright, hopeful smile I remembered from long ago.
"I can help your business grow!" she wrote in bold letters, above her
smiling face.

I stared at Polina's beaming picture from our college days, wondering if I, too, had been conned by her bright smile.

* * *

Polina and I were transferred to a ladies-only dorm for our sophomore
year, and though we remained friends, we began to move in different
crowds. I was making more friends in the English department and
meeting young writers at literary events while she began to hang out
with a particular crowd that I tried to avoid. I'd be taking a shower
when one of her new friends moaned loudly for Jesus in the next stall
through the sound of falling water. Another friend of hers would be
leaning against the rails of our open-air corridor, ranting about an aunt
who refused to accept Jesus as her personal Lord and Savior. Polina
had attended Bible study sessions in our freshman year, but none of

it resulted in the Bible-thumping fervency that alienated me from her new friends. While my fear of their religiosity cut me off from our dorm's community life, which was gleefully dominated by their prayer meetings, Polina gravitated toward these women, perhaps finding in their company a kind of validation even I could not give her.

I may have cracked a joke or two at our dorm socials to ease my discomfort when they started talking about their on-campus revivals, for they began to glare at me as I walked down the corridors of our dorm. Though Polina still stopped by my room every so often to chat, she'd avoid me when her new friends were around. There was something about me, perhaps the way I talked about sex, or maybe the way I described the obscene foreign-language films I watched at our university film center, that seemed to frighten her. Was she afraid of catching something from me, or was she merely listening to her new friends, who raised their disdainful eyes at me as I walked past their Bible study meetings?

I noticed a subtle change when she called out to the Lord over a particularly difficult homework assignment and when she lent her enthusiastic assent to a girl's story about a "brother" who had been blessed by the Lord with a sparkling new mansion. I continued to feel lost and adrift during our sophomore year and couldn't approach life with the same certainty that these women possessed. Would it have helped if I did? Whenever Polina returned, flushed and delirious, from a revival, I asked myself if the euphoria she felt was worth her complete surrender to her new faith, or if she'd come to depend on religion like an addict needing her fix.

"They keep calling out to the Lord, but all they want from him are new cars and refrigerators," I blurted out one day, as we sat across from each other in our communal study room. I don't remember what provoked this outburst, but I remember thinking that she was better than this, and that I needed to pull her away before it was too late.

"Is this what it's all about?" I asked. Was I getting through to her as she stared at the table, as though receiving a scolding?

"Worshipping him so that you can get what you want, without having to do anything good in return?"

To this, she said nothing.

* * *

Perhaps it's presumptuous of me to believe it was within my powers to keep her safe from the choices she made when it's obvious to me now that my opinions held no weight within her constellation of beliefs. And yet I wonder if what she needed from me was not a warning but rather the reassurances that only my future self could have given her, that she, and I, had what it took to face life's uncertainties on our own, without having to take refuge in the false promises of religious fundamentalism or get-rich-quick schemes. Perhaps this wisdom can only be acquired in hindsight, after years of living. And yet I remain unsettled in this knowledge.

I keep returning to the evening of my eighteenth birthday, when Polina met me outside my dorm room in a pretty dress. We chatted excitedly as we walked to the fancy restaurant I had chosen for my party, as she allowed me to lead her into a secluded bistro behind a grove of trees before she came to a stop beneath its arched entrance, her voice softening with awe as she looked upward at the lights strung above our heads. Later that evening, as a little cake with a candle was brought in by a waiter to the cheers of my friends, she congratulated me for the woman I had become and the person I was yet to become. She was the most articulate in our group of friends from freshman year, and I wasn't surprised when she gave this impromptu speech capturing the heady feeling enveloping us all. In the company of these women, it was impossible for me to doubt Polina's words.

"It's like the stars have come out for you on your special day," she told me later that evening, as we stood on our dorm's rooftop deck, as though offering ourselves up to the moon and the starlit sky. She talked about the miracle of my birth and the promising future I had, and none of it sounded trite or fake as we stood beneath those stars. With Polina, I found it easier to believe that the future, which neither of us had the power to see, remained bright.

Katherine Mansfield's Light

Near the beginning of her story "Prelude," Katherine Mansfield makes one brief mention of Quarantine Island in Wellington Harbor. The Burnell family are moving from their house near the center of town to a more sprawling property in the country, and Lottie and Kezia, their two youngest daughters, are the last to leave. It is evening when they set out in a buggy sent for them, and it is the first time they have been out so late; excitedly, they turn back toward the neighborhood where they have spent their entire lives, noticing how much smaller its familiar houses seem in the darkness, before seeing the stars in the night sky and the moon hanging over the harbor. It is at this point that they notice Quarantine Island's lighthouse shining in the middle of the bay.

Though Mansfield does not dwell on this detail—choosing instead to follow the girls as their buggy reaches the top of a hill before they lose sight of the harbor altogether—the image of a lone, shining island in the middle of a glimmering bay anchors the rest of this scene, for it is where the overarching sense of hush evoked by the night sky, the city lights, the stars, the moon, and the gold-tinged waves comes to rest.

* * *

I probably wouldn't have recognized Mansfield's Quarantine Island as the Matiu Island I knew from my Wellington days if I hadn't visited myself, and if Vincent and I hadn't found the old cemetery for victims of the so-called "Spanish flu" pandemic near its tiny port. One has to veer slightly off the main trail encircling the island to find the cemetery, tucked behind native bush. Some of its headstones are so tall that they tower over scrub grass, and if one has a look at them, they'll note the names of siblings and their ages etched down each stone in the order of their deaths. Many of the dead were children, and I wonder how it felt for Vincent, who had immigrated to New Zealand at an early age, to stumble upon the graves of children who had likewise arrived in this country with their parents only to meet their deaths before their ships could dock in Wellington. Some died within the same day, some within the same week; some had parents whose names accompanied theirs on their family headstone, which also bore the name of the ship that had carried them to this small island on the other side of the world.

"There were so many incurable diseases back then, so people died young," I remember Vincent saying, as we stared at names and dates from a distant time. The day's unrelenting sunshine made us feel as though the tragedies that had befallen those buried beneath our feet belonged to a faraway era, and within the safety of the present we dedicated a brief moment of silence for the dead. But soon we were making our way back to the main trail, toward the island's summit, where our eyes ached from staring at the endless, glittering water as we talked about a future that seemed just as bright when glimpsed from afar.

* * *

Visible from much of the city and the surrounding hills, Matiu Island is an everyday sight for Wellingtonians, occupying a permanent though peripheral presence in their lives. Even before the Spanish flu pandemic of 1918, the island was used as a quarantine station for immigrants from Europe entering New Zealand aboard infected ships. Judging by her gentle description of the island in "Prelude," I can imagine Mansfield growing up in its proximity, finding its presence quietly reassuring even when glimpsed from afar, despite its reputation for harboring foreignness and disease.

Perhaps it was my nostalgia for New Zealand that led me to pick up my secondhand copy of Mansfield's selected stories when much of the Philippines was placed under lockdown. I was about to leave for an artists' residency in Japan when the airports were closed, and in a single day our movements became regulated and monitored in ways I never could have imagined a few days earlier. Our neighborhood, or barangay, had a loudspeaker broadcasting orders from officials to stay at home; whenever we left our barangay to buy groceries or medicine, we had to pass by the barangay office and tell them where we were going before we could be issued a quarantine pass. Checkpoints were everywhere, with armed police inspecting our quarantine passes before allowing us to proceed. I'd be buying imported chocolates to cheer myself up only to overhear the grocery clerk telling her boss on a walkie-talkie what I was purchasing.

At home with my mother, our days grew simple, unburdened of priorities that seemed to belong, as time wore on, to a different life. My thoughts were no longer directed toward a vague and uncertain future but toward the present, the everyday, as I strove to maintain my sanity within the confines of domestic life. In New Zealand, no such restrictions had been put in place yet, and my mind often returned to what my life had been like before I returned to my home country, which seemed to be slipping deeper into authoritarian rule.

I had purchased my copy of Mansfield's selected stories at a used bookshop in Wellington shortly after I defended my PhD thesis, intending to read it upon my return to the Philippines. Her patient and detailed style felt too ponderous, however, and I quickly moved on to contemporary fiction, promising myself that I'd eventually give Mansfield another go, when I had the time for her. It was the COVID-19 quarantine, in the end, that would force me to slow down, to pay attention to Mansfield's words while the threat of disease kept me rooted in my childhood home, unable to flee.

As the streets of our neighborhood emptied out, the sound of birdsong began to emerge through the growing hush that held us still. I took to sitting on our front balcony in the mornings, reading Mansfield's stories, pausing every now and then to observe birds flitting through our bougainvillea bushes. Tiny green buds emerged from the bare branches of our guava tree, which had appeared on the brink of death before lockdown began. Life continued at its usual pace in our garden, urging blossoms forth, drawing butterflies and birds to the flora surrounding our house.

Like life in the garden, Mansfield's stories unfold at a leisurely pace, taking in the way light falls across a lawn or gleams through morning mist, or how a flower with a tiny tongue at its center seems to be so lovingly shaped that it is "such a waste" for it to wither and fall onto the ground. One of my writer friends once told me that reading Mansfield's work was an unpleasant experience for many Kiwis, who were forced to read her stories in high school, and I can see why her work would tax a teenager's patience. Mansfield's stories draw their narrative pacing from the unhurried pulse of everyday life; one must recalibrate one's sense of narrative time so that one can appreciate the description of "a green wandering light playing over" a cup of coffee, or of a café proprietor whose longing pose beside a window seems to have become an unconscious habit. I can imagine her stories being tossed aside by editors of contemporary literary journals because of descriptions and scenes that could read as labored, inessential, or overindulgent to a reader today. Accustomed to trimming away what we deem unnecessary in the service of more efficient, "urgent" storytelling, perhaps we have lost the capacity to appreciate the rewards of a meandering description of a beach, or of a room in an abandoned house.

Mansfield's stories require a childlike sense of wonder. Readers must find magic in details grown-ups too often take for granted, such as the little almond doorknob in a gingerbread house that a young boy cannot stop thinking about in "Sun and Moon," or the little lamp inside a doll's house that Kezia keeps describing to her schoolmates in "The Doll's House." At a time when we are forced to slow down, to think in the present tense instead of hankering for what is yet to be, I wonder if Mansfield is the writer we need, when our future feels uncertain and the present is all we can truly claim for ourselves.

* * *

"Prelude" was written a few years before the Spanish flu pandemic, but the story takes place much earlier in history. Inspired by her brother's visits to her London home, Mansfield began to write about her childhood in New Zealand, and time and distance were enough to soften her memories of a homeland whose narrow-mindedness and provincialism she had once chafed against. The Burnells closely resemble her own family, the Beauchamps, who also moved their young family from a smaller house in town to a larger property in Karori. Kezia, the more observant and imaginative of the three sisters in the story, may be a stand-in for Mansfield herself. Mansfield's antipathy toward her family, expressed overtly in her letters, is absent in "Prelude" but appears, in a gentler form, in subsequent stories about the Burnells such as "At the Bay" and "The Doll's House." Her depictions of family life are lovingly detailed, employing descriptions of the smallest gestures, mannerisms, and endearments to paint a portrait of the Burnells that radiates with longing for the innocence of childhood and the safety of home.

Leslie, Mansfield's younger brother, was among the many young New Zealand men conscripted by the British to fight in World War I. Leslie had many opportunities to visit his sister in London while he trained as an officer in England, and the memories they shared during his visits awakened a longing in Mansfield for her homeland and youth—a longing that found full expression in a story titled "The Aloe," which was to become "Prelude." Her disappointment in her family and homeland was indeed justified: her parents did not exactly appreciate her literary ambitions, and her mother, worried that Mansfield was exhibiting signs of same-sex attraction, once sailed all the way from New Zealand to England to take her to a small town in Germany, where she allegedly underwent what is now known as gay conversion therapy. But Mansfield adored her brother, and the childhood they shared, by all accounts, was a happy one. Much of Mansfield's earlier fiction is set in Europe, but Leslie's visits offered her the possibility of reclaiming a past that was lost to her when she left for England, and of re-creating in her fiction a cherished New Zealand she could claim as her own.

It was grief, in the end, that fueled her completion of "Prelude," for Leslie was killed in Belgium in October 1915. She began writing "The Aloe" after his death, and I can imagine the urgency she felt as she wrestled with the permanence of his passing and the loss of their shared past. Reading "Prelude" in 2020, amid a pandemic that has led me to contemplate the nearness of death in ways I'd never before thought necessary, I feel as though the story taunts mortality by showing us what death cannot fully take away: the Wellington of Mansfield and her brother's childhood is intact on the page, as is the feeling of innocence that remains unmarred throughout the story by the petty squabbles and concerns of adults. Death, in the form of a duck's surprise slaughter in front of the children, or the image of Quarantine Island shining at night, hovers on the periphery but does not bring the story, with all its disparate and fascinating characters, to a complete pause.

* * *

The unending tragedies playing on a reel as my mother and I consumed the news made the unusual stillness that filled our days feel immobilizing. While I was reading Mansfield at a leisurely pace on our balcony, doctors were dying of the disease; their beaming faces would flash on our TV screen as we learned about their ages, their specializations, their tireless work on the front lines. There was a cardiologist admired by many in his field; a barrio doctor who had dedicated his entire career to serving the poor; a pediatrician who had closely monitored the disease's spread in the Philippines before she herself fell ill; and a pediatric surgeon who was the only doctor in our country capable of separating conjoined twins, who loved riding his motorcycle around the countryside whenever he had a free day. There was a husband and wife, both doctors, who fell ill and were kept apart from each other as they fought for their lives; the husband fought hard before succumbing to the disease because he was afraid that there would be no one to care for his autistic son.

Meanwhile, our president, Rodrigo Duterte, delivered meandering late-night speeches peppered with insults and threats aimed at those who dared break the quarantine. In one speech, he told the police to shoot violators; the next day, a man who had lost his patience at a checkpoint and fought with the police was shot dead. In another speech, the president proclaimed that the doctors who had died on the front lines were lucky to die for their country, adding, "If it's your time to go, then it's your time to go."

A flight evacuating a COVID-19 patient to Japan burst into flames during takeoff in Manila, killing everyone on board. A young doctor was on this flight, and shortly before boarding he posted on social media that he couldn't wait for the pandemic to end. He was my age, just a year younger than Mansfield herself when she died of tuberculosis at thirty-four.

It was at this point that I began to wonder if it was possible to grow numb from despair.

* * *

Mansfield was diagnosed with tuberculosis near the end of World War I. Her doctor advised her to give up writing so that she could live a longer life, thinking it best for her to reserve her bodily strength for fighting the disease. Her writing consumed much of her energy, but it was something she was unwilling to surrender, even to live. Giving death full control over her life was a kind of death in itself; it wasn't the life Mansfield wanted to live. In her earlier work, death hovers at the corner of one's eye, a constant yet peripheral presence in the lives of characters who have grown indifferent to its shadows despite its occasional and brief intimations. Most of the time, the brightness of life is an overwhelming presence in itself, especially for the children in her stories, who are just beginning to understand the world in which they live. Death is a part of this world, but life, in its infinite brightness, outshines it.

It was during this period, in which she traveled from resort town to resort town in Europe in search of a cure for her illness, that Mansfield turned again to her childhood in New Zealand, which seemed far removed from the darkness and pain that now overshadowed her life. She wrote vividly about her homeland, most notably in her stories "At the Bay" and "The Doll's House," in which the Burnells reappear, as they do in the loosely autobiographical "The Garden Party," which takes place in Mansfield's childhood neighborhood of Thorndon. Absent from these stories is the kind of cynicism one would expect from a writer who knows she will die young. The same sense of childhood wonderment present in her earlier work suffuses the descriptions and characterizations in these later stories. Her impending death leant a greater urgency to recording life exactly as it presented itself to her—to preserve its sharpness and vividness even as death, finally impossible to ignore, asserted its presence more clearly. It is referenced in a conversation Kezia has with her grandmother in "At the Bay," in which she asks why her uncle William died young before wondering aloud if everyone must die. And in "The Garden Party," Laura directly confronts the indifference of her wealthy family when a workman is killed in an accident just below their garden—she is told that their garden party must go on, that they cannot allow the death of a man they don't know to ruin their happiness.

Society's inability to accommodate grieving and loss also comes to the fore in Mansfield's later work. In "Life of Ma Parker," an old servant mourning the death of a beloved grandchild finds no solace in her writer employer's voyeuristic interest in her suffering, while in "The Fly," a businessman is unexpectedly forced to reckon with his grief over losing his son six years before, and without a proper outlet for his emotions, he finds a fly on his desk and slowly tortures it to death. There also seems to be a greater amount of honesty surrounding casual cruelty in Mansfield's later work: in "The Doll's House," for instance, she unflinchingly portrays the cruelty of children in a schoolyard as they gang up on the daughters of a washerwoman. Insulting the Kelvey girls by telling them they're going to become servants when they grow up gives the other girls such a rush that "never did they skip so high, run in and out so fast, or do such daring things as on this morning." Cruelty seems to coexist more closely with innocence and goodness in the later work, to the point that these qualities often coexist within a single character: the Burnells' Aunt Beryl, for instance, is shown to be a sensitive and perceptive woman in "At the Bay," while in "The Doll's House" she shoos the Kelvey sisters away from the Burnells' front yard "as if they were chickens," having caught Kezia showing them the doll's house that was never meant for their eyes. Guarding one's innocence against the cruelties of the world, a recurring theme in Mansfield's earlier work, becomes a seemingly impossible undertaking in these later stories.

And yet there remains a certain optimism in the later stories that allows for the celebration of goodness in the face of cruelty, even when it is tempting to be cynical about the lasting effects of kindness in a cruel world. The girls in "The Doll's House" ostracize the Kelvey sisters because they are told by their parents not to play with them, and their parents, who look down on Mrs. Kelvey and suspect her husband is in jail, view the Kelveys' "moral dereliction" as a contagious disease that their children could contract through close association. It is Kezia's innocence that renders her immune to the prejudices of her parents and peers, allowing her to invite the Kelveys to her family's front yard, where the doll's house is on display, because she doesn't see why the Kelvey sisters shouldn't see this precious little house with its treasured little lamp she has told the entire school about. In the end, it is Kezia's kindness that the two girls remember, not "the cross lady": they trade smiles by the side of the road after Aunt Beryl shoos them away, and Else says, "I seen the little lamp."

* * *

My small moments of joy in this difficult time are often accompanied by guilt: I am not on the front lines of the pandemic, where the real battles are being fought. I am fortunate to count myself among the middle class of a third-world country during a lockdown that has become increasingly punitive toward the poor and has left many of its citizens to starve. It is indeed tempting to give in to a creeping sense of futility when none of us know when, or if, this pandemic will end, especially when it continues to take the lives of the best and kindest among us.

But then I think about the way Mansfield lived in the presence of death, and how the recognition of her own mortality allowed her to write honestly about death, even as life, and human kindness, continued to shine through her work. I find it impossible to ignore the light her stories have given me access to during this pandemic, especially when the alternative is giving in to the nihilism and callousness perpetuated by our president in his nightly speeches. I want to honor the lives of the doctors and nurses who have died fighting this pandemic, so I cannot give in to despair. If their deaths are to have any meaning, this world for which they sacrificed their lives must contain some kindness, some light.

* * *

As I seek to tread carefully between joy and mourning, wishing to honor both without negating either, I wonder if it is possible to find sanctuary in my own happiness without becoming numb to the tragedies taking place around me. Guarding my own happiness is the only way I can persevere, but how to do this without pushing away my grief, also necessary for my healing?

Among the stories I've read by Mansfield, "The Garden Party" has given me the most solace in the midst of death and despair. A worker is killed in an accident below the Sheridans' garden, and while Laura feels it is inappropriate to continue with the garden party her family has been preparing for weeks, her sister and mother dismiss her pleas to call it off. Mrs. Sheridan tells her, "People like that don't expect sacrifices from us. And it's not very sympathetic to spoil everybody's enjoyment as you're doing now," while her sister Jose says, "You won't bring a drunken workman back to life by being sentimental."

Despite Laura's protests, the party goes on as planned, and while Laura continues to think about the dead man whose family inhabits one of the "little mean dwellings" on a street leading up to their house, she also basks in the perfection of the afternoon as she receives compliments for her beauty from guests, and enjoys the music played by a hired band whose cheery sound she had worried would bring pain to the dead man's grieving widow.

After their guests leave, Mr. Sheridan mentions the man's death and the family he has left behind and is immediately censured by his wife: "'My dear,' said Mrs. Sheridan, holding up her hand, 'It nearly ruined the party. Laura insisted we should put it off.'" For a passing moment, even Laura finds her father tactless for mentioning the man's death, quickly catching herself when her mother comes up with the idea of collecting leftovers from the party in a basket for the grieving family, in addition to some arum lilies, because "People of that class are so impressed by arum lilies."

Carrying the basket, Laura descends the hill toward the dead man's house, and while she had merely intended to leave the basket outside his door, to her horror she is pulled inside when his family answers the door. While the Sheridans are determined to keep the squalor of the impoverished neighborhood adjacent to their property at bay, the dead man's family seems intent on bringing Laura into their world and exposing the rawness of their grief to her. Even as Laura tries to escape, the dead man's sister invites her into the bedroom where the dead man is lying, drawing away the sheet covering his face for Laura to see:

> There lay a young man, fast asleep—sleeping so soundly, so deeply, that he was far, far away from them both. Oh, so remote, so peaceful. He was dreaming. Never wake him up

again. His head was sunk in the pillow, his eyes were closed; they were blind under the closed eyelids. He was given up to his dream. What did garden-parties and baskets and lace frocks matter to him? He was far from all those things. He was wonderful, beautiful. While they were laughing and while the band was playing, this marvel had come to the lane. Happy . . . happy . . . All is well, said that sleeping face. This is just as it should be. I am content.

"It was simply marvelous," Laura tells her brother upon her return. She tries to explain what she has seen, but no words can capture what she has come to understand about life just by glimpsing the dead man's face.

She has seen life's beauty in its fullest form, and she has also felt its ache.

My Father and Yadi

Yadi, a large brown bear with soft eyes, a button nose, and a ready smile, appears in many of my childhood photos. As a toddler I often held him close, for he was my shield, my comfort animal. In one photo, he is seated before me on the floor, and I'm wearing an apron, holding a shopping bag aloft while staring into space. Perhaps, like my father, I was a writer even then, easily absorbed by worlds of my own making.

As a toddler, I took a liking for the letter Y, calling water "yebo," my beloved teddy bear "Yadi." My father latched on to the name Yadi, perhaps because it was my own creation—he wrote in English, spinning words borrowed from a foreign tongue. He was amazed by how I held on to my invented words even as I began to learn Tagalog and English, as though my words carried private meanings that were mine alone to savor and keep. The things that gave me comfort as a child, my father loved as well, and he would continue to cherish my invented language, along with Yadi, long after I had outgrown them.

In one picture, my curls have grown to a voluptuous length, and my eyes are wet as I hold Yadi close. The picture was taken in Manila the evening before we flew to America. In pictures taken after this move, my father often towers over me, or holds me in his lap in our small apartment. He is my protector, my playmate whenever my mother is away. Yadi is in some of these pictures, though I'm taller than Yadi now, and I treat him as one of my many toys rather than as my protector. My smile and expression gradually open up in these pictures—not only am I growing up, I am also becoming an American. There is one picture in which my father holds Yadi in his lap—Yadi seems like his surrogate child who won't grow up, while his daughter, once Yadi's best friend, keeps growing.

Due to luggage restrictions, we had to leave Yadi with my aunt when we returned to the Philippines. But during the next twelve years of Yadi's "exile," the bear acquired a mythic significance in our family, especially for my father, who pined with me for the bear's return.

* * *

I had just graduated from college when my aunt finally visited the Philippines with Yadi in tow. This time, he felt small in my arms, and my parents were astonished by how tiny he seemed when he had once dwarfed me. Yadi was the baby now, and my father would pick him up and hug him every now and then, like a parent reassuring himself that his long-lost child was truly home. I was working in another city by this time, but Yadi, who remained childlike with his ready, frozen smile, would never grow old.

My father loved me, which was why he respected my freedom—he knew his love would shelter me from harm, no matter how far I traveled to reach my dreams. When I left the Philippines again, Yadi would stay behind instead of coming with me. Every once in a while, my father would ask my mother, who was more technologically adept, to text me that "he had hugged Yadi for me." Whenever I'd receive these messages, half a world away, I would feel his embrace—I was an adult now, but in many ways I was still my father's little girl.

Yadi could have accompanied me, of course, but during one visit, my father told me that it was better for Yadi to stay. "You should come home and visit him once in a while," he said, smiling as he patted Yadi. It was through these small gestures that my father admitted to me that he missed me, though he never kept me from leaving.

We kept in close touch, Yadi serving as a helpful go-between, allowing my father to articulate his love for me in ways that weren't saccharine or trite. On a cold morning in July, my mother texted me that my father had wrapped Yadi in an embroidered malong blanket to keep him warm, because it was getting cold at home. Far away, in wintry Wellington, I could feel the warmth of my father's touch.

Two weeks later, I got another text from my mother. I had to come home immediately, she'd written. My father was dead.

When I arrived home, I hugged Yadi again, wondering, in my childlike way, if he missed my father as much as I did. "Who's going to hug you now?" I asked Yadi, my tears falling on his glass eyes.

Years after my father's passing, Yadi sits in his usual corner in our alcove, his large, flattened head slumped over his fading body. When I remember to hug him, hoping that the bear feels less lonely, I can almost feel my father's embrace, his longing for my eventual return.

Disappearing Houses

My mother tells me there was once a small, American-style clapboard home on the opposite side of our glen where a large and ugly warehouse now stands. She says the home remained vacant much of the year, except in the summer months, but that even when its wealthy owners were away, caretakers living in the adjacent house tended to its lush, terraced garden. When the owners passed away, their children sold the property to a businessman who demolished the house, leveled the hill on which it stood, and built the warehouse in its place. The warehouse was a constant source of grief for my father, who had first seen the old house when he came to our city as a young man—I can still recall him throwing dismayed glances at the warehouse's graying façade, his face souring as though contemplating a stubborn old stain.

"That wasn't there before," he'd mutter, frowning. "And now it dwarfs everything."

Now, from our balcony, I watch men carry stacks of boxes on their backs into the warehouse's cavernous entrance. In this pandemic, time seems to have ceased to penetrate our days, leaving us stranded within a single, repeating scene. But the passage of time has left its mark on the warehouse's beige façade; its paint has begun to peel, exposing a sickly gray surface the owner tried to hide with a paint job and crisscrossing planks, artlessly imitating the exposed timber of a Tudor-style home. Built before I was born, its appearance does not evoke the past: its large, dark windows are grilled, suggesting an impersonal hollowness within its hulking body.

* * *

Returning to the Philippines after my father's death felt easier than
staying on overseas and finding a job; it was easier for me to collapse
into my own grief surrounded by the familiar. But I had no intention
of staying in Baguio, and before the pandemic, I traveled overseas
periodically, mainly for artists' residencies. These trips reassured me
of the ties I maintained to the outside world, despite the easiness with
which I yielded to the pull of home.

My father, too, maintained a complicated relationship with our
city after moving here to join my mother in the early 1980s. Before
coming to Baguio, he had been a full-time professor at a public university in Mindanao, but he could only find temporary work at the
university where my mother taught. My parents would erupt into
fights in the middle of the night when I was a child, my father digging up his resentments over leaving his home in Mindanao, moving
far away from his friends and colleagues who had recognized his abilities. "This isn't my home," I'd hear him repeat to my mother as I lay
in bed, struggling to fall asleep.

The next morning, when I emerged from my bedroom, I'd find
my father sitting in a chair in our living room, waiting to speak to
me. "If you came with me to Mindanao," he'd tell me, as my mother
dozed in their bedroom, "you'd meet your cousins, and I'd be a full
professor."

Though I told myself that I'd follow my father anywhere that
offered him the happiness he found so elusive in our city, I wasn't sure
if I was ready to leave the world I knew. Moving back to the Philippines from America when I was eight had shaken me; another move
to Mindanao, where I'd have to learn a new language and would be
so far away from my mother, likely wouldn't have been as simple as
my father made it seem.

In my company, he'd express his antipathy for Baguio: its intel-
lectuals were standoffish and status conscious, its writers more
concerned with gaining the approval of the city's elite than paying
serious attention to their craft. Its leaders had no vision for the future
of the city, according to him, cutting down pine trees and demolish-
ing American colonial-era homes in the name of progress, advertising

its cooler temperatures and colonial history to tourists without having any interest in making the city more livable for its inhabitants.

But when I was old enough to read and understand my father's poetry, I could sense in it an awed recognition of the magical qualities that our city possessed, making me curious if beneath all his criticisms lurked a reverence for a city that wasn't receiving the care it deserved. One only has to read his poem about a Catholic seminary located on the outskirts of Baguio, "Return to Maryhurst," to see how a place that broke his heart also ensnared him in its enchantments:

> The land launches out like a ramp
> Into the open sky, into the sun,
> Then drops and flows way down
> Into the distant blue valleys and hills below
> That dance like the waves of a sunken, uneven sea,
> Too far down to reach, to lap this ledge,
> This quay that obtrudes, confronts—
> And the strand behind it that the wind blasts
> As though coming in from the farthest reaches
> To pour in notice of strength gathered, seemingly,
> From a trove of infinite resources,
> Combing the grass back so close
> To its skull of earth such that a few blooms
> Wiggle their way out of being broken,
> Though the rest arch tautly backward
> Like catapults, the flower-heads softest of missiles
> That spring forward *en masse*,
> As, suddenly, the wind drops.

We visited this garden together when I was in high school, and I remember my parents pointing out spots where a flowering plant or shrub once stood, noting to each other how a particular winding path carved along the hillside seemed lusher and more vibrant when they were younger. The years had brought a proliferation of headstones in the seminary's graveyard, each bearing the name of a priest who had come here to spend his final days. Was it the exuberance of youth, perhaps, that had sharpened their memories of this hillside garden?

Or was it the weariness of age that made them pine for a fresher, more radiant past?

> Memory and presence jostle for position, now,
> The past emerging from behind,
> Pentimentally possessive
> While each presence
> Is pushed back to the past,
> Assumed to have been there
> When we were there,
> Although some confusion dissipates
> When we pause to think of ourselves in time,
> And then confront the same insistent sun, wind, Space,
> Not as we used to be but as we are.

But how do I retrace the steps to what my father saw in his youth, now that shiny new condominiums have encroached on the pine forests that once surrounded Maryhurst? My parents understood that the city was changing, erasing its past with each garden and landmark bulldozed to make way for a hotel or parking lot. I ask myself if the seminary and its sprawling garden are likewise bound to fall into the hands of unscrupulous developers. I do not share my father's self-assurance when he wrote,

> The garden of earth holds just as firmly
> As once it had when arm in arm
> We pushed forward to the garden's edge.

How do I find the footing he discovered in such rare moments of peace, when the hidden corners of Baguio that astonished him into silence have begun to disappear before my eyes? I came back to Baguio to ease my torment after my father's passing, but even the parts of our city that kept him rooted here have a tenuous grip on the land, and in our memories.

* * *

During my father's wake, I found myself growing mute with rage as well-meaning guests took it upon themselves to remind me of my obligation to finish my PhD quickly and return home from New Zealand to care for my grieving mother. My own anguish was just another inconvenience they brushed aside as they lectured me on my duties as a daughter, and I felt myself disappearing before them, my ghost searching the room for my father. Without him, I felt no real reason to stay.

I returned to Wellington, where life went on as it did before my father's passing. A middle-aged white woman at my PhD program, who seemed to enjoy questioning me about "the dire situation" in my country, asked me upon my return if we welcomed visitors to our home after we buried my father so that we could "have some fun after all that." She was writing a novel about the battered wives of a developing nation whose rituals and customs she described in vivid, patronizing prose, and I imagined she pictured my mother and I dancing around a fire and yelling gibberish inside a circle of bongo-banging guests. Another classmate, who had disinvited me from a reading after I called out her racism in a workshop, asked me on my first day back at the office if I was relieved "to be far away from all of that." It seemed so easy for these people to fit my grief inside a compact box, to file it away in the furthermost corners of their minds.

A pleasant elderly Filipino man, whose small downtown dough-nut shop I frequented for Filipino pastries and friendly conversation, offered me his condolences before launching into a tirade about how my father's death was written in the book of God, and that in reject-ing God's law, I was rejecting God. "You need to listen to me because this will help you," he pleaded as I walked away, before yelling after me, "I'm praying for you."

Not every person I met was unkind: I had friends who made me feel less alone in my sadness by listening as I raged and grieved, paying attention instead of dismissing my pain. Strangers I met in unexpected places could also be kind, like a Swedish woman I met at a conference in Hamilton, an inland city on New Zealand's North Island, who listened to me talk about my father and described to me the energies and love that transcended death before allowing me to weep into her chest.

"New Zealand is a beautiful country," she said over pizza and drinks, after inviting me to dinner with another new friend. "Traveling will help you."

I took trips away from Wellington, allowing the beauty of New Zealand's lakes, sounds, and forests to sweep over me, as though responding to and acknowledging the immensity of my sorrow. The more I honored my grief, the more I felt its heaviness lifting. I knew I had to go on mourning to make my way back to the light, and so I returned to Baguio, hoping to find my moorings in the town my father and I reluctantly called home.

* * *

In the early 1980s, while waiting for my mother to return from her graduate studies in the United States, my father befriended a group of visual artists whose work often depicted scenes from everyday life in our city. Together they formed an artists' collective called the Tahong Bundok, which roughly translates to "men from the mountains," adjusting their rules to accommodate my father, who was the only writer in the group. Much of their time together was spent drinking, singing, talking about books, and hiking up Baguio's empty hills. One particular hill they loved to climb was Quirino Hill, which had huge boulders to grab on when they struggled with its steep incline and groves of sunflowers that my father's friends sketched in their notebooks when they reached the hill's summit. Whenever we drove past it, it didn't quite match the picture in my mind of the rocky, grassy hill my father had so often described in his stories, for every inch of it seemed covered in concrete and ramshackle housing. "The sunflowers are gone now," my father would say, his voice trailing off as his eyes searched for what was no longer there. He would then add, "You'll see the sunflowers in their paintings, but that's about it."

He'd take me to the Tahong Bundok studio managed by his good friend, Pyx Picart, and the two would sit down to share gossip over instant coffee in the unpretentious little gallery that moved from one downtown location to another. Paintings would be crammed onto the walls, and though some were of sunflowers, there was much more: there were mothers carrying babies in handwoven slings or talking to their children in doorways and old, wrinkly women husking rice in wooden pestles. Pyx Picart, a native son of Baguio, had many stories to share about the city's founding families, whose closets were full of skeletons, and of the American colonial schools that were now long gone. When Pyx was busy entertaining other guests, my father would rise from his seat and take me to see Pyx's paintings. Amid the portraits of city life, Pyx's work stood out: when I saw his paintings of weeping willows cascading through the soft gleam of Burnham Park's man-made lake, I knew I wasn't just looking at a scene, but that I was sinking back into a moment I might've experienced in the past but had forgotten. The Burnham Park I knew was grimy, crowded, and smelled of garbage and piss, but in Pyx's paintings there were no extraneous details to pull me away from the recesses of memory. The scenes felt so familiar to me in their quiet gleaming, even though I had never seen Burnham Park like this.

As I grew older, my father confessed to me that Pyx was his only real friend in Baguio, and so whenever Pyx had a falling out with any of the Tahong Bundok members, my father would always take Pyx's side. "He's a difficult person, but he sees things that the rest of them can't see," my father would say, when I pointed out to him how Pyx sometimes spoke unkindly of other artists behind their backs and often complained. But Pyx would clear his worktable whenever my father wanted to write poetry in his gallery, knowing perhaps that a man who remained loyal to him because of his art was also a person who had important things to say about the world. "He's the one person in this town, aside from you and your mama, who gets what I'm doing," my father said. "Without him, I don't know what would've become of me in this godforsaken town."

Shortly after my father died, the city began renovations on the government building that housed Pyx's gallery, and as Pyx prepared to leave his home one morning, he found his paintings, books, and personal computer dumped outside his gate. "They just broke the lock and threw everything out," he moaned, as we sat across from each other at a downtown café, his knobby fingers tensing around his coffee cup as though grasping at what was no longer there. Shaking his head, he said, "They just didn't care."

* * *

When we returned home from America, the hilltop beyond our glen was covered in pine trees, and I now try to picture what I saw as a child from our house, before the pitched roofs of a condominium complex took the place of those treetops. My parents enrolled me in a small private school right next to this grove of trees, and I remember staring down at it from our classroom window, feeling submerged in my own confused thoughts amid these children who all looked like me but spoke only to each other and teased me in a language I couldn't understand. My only friend was a blonde Eurasian named Elizabeth who, like me, couldn't speak Tagalog, and I'd picture the two of us in our green checkered uniforms running hand in hand through the pine forest, away from our teachers who misunderstood us and our classmates who yelled at us to "go back to America" whenever we wanted to play with them. When I returned to school after the summer break to learn that Elizabeth and her family had moved to Malaysia, I again found myself looking out from our classroom window at the rambling, tree-covered ridge beneath us, feeling myself being pulled into its depths as I dreamed of escape.

When the bulldozers rolled in, accompanied by men carrying chainsaws, my classmates crowded around the school's windows, letting out excited yelps when each towering pine tree came crashing down from the sky into the red earth. I couldn't bear to look at it, but there were times when I'd glance at the clearing below, silently reciting a prayer for the trees that still stood. At that age, I hadn't yet fully experienced how one's prayers could fall on deaf ears; it was probably my earliest lesson on the futility of faith. One couldn't just will a forest—or a friend—to remain.

"A thousand trees cut down, for condo units that nobody lives in," my father said whenever we walked past the buildings that rose in their place. My parents transferred me to another private school, down the street from our house, the following year, and thereafter I didn't have to walk past the towering condo buildings with their tacky pine tree–accented eaves and window frames on my way to school. But the enchantments of Brent Road, with its grand vacation homes nestled beneath towering pines, continued to exert their pull on us, and my father and I would sometimes take walks all the way to the end of the street, where Brent School's guard house barred common folk like us from its wooded campus. We'd turn around, passing the green-and-white American colonial home that housed my former school before walking past what used to be a pine forest, which was now a housing complex called the Pineridge. Two scraggly Norfolk pines flanked its gated entrance that was patrolled by a uniformed guard. I tried to picture the bungalow that once sat at a short distance from the sidewalk and the cheerful man whom I saw emerging from its door with his two children each morning, who wore the same checkered green uniform as me. An entire pine forest had risen behind their wooden house, also painted green, easing itself into the greenery to which it belonged. Had I dreamed this scene up? No trace of it remained in the condo towers or in the paved streets that snaked around them. There was only the halfhearted effort to evoke the idea of a "pine ridge" in the building's faux pine accents, and in the Norfolk pines evenly spaced around the grounds like Christmas decorations in a department store. There was nothing in this bland design that echoed the dark pull of the forest that had wrapped itself around my heart when I was a child.

"At least it's nice looking," I said to my father, when we saw it for the first time. Was I attempting to console myself? I had seen uglier buildings go up in our city, such as the warehouse that faced our home.

My father made a face. "All those trees cut down for buildings only rich people can live in."

From our own house, we'd see the slate roofs rising through a thicket of trees, replacing what we remembered to be a dense patch of green with what appeared like the rooftops of luxury chalets. Their design was so conciliatory, blending in so seamlessly with the greenery that remained further down the hill, that I began to forget what the forest had once looked like. Was I correct in remembering that it would turn bluish at times, if the late afternoon light filtered through its branches in a certain way? My memories had nothing to anchor themselves to, and as more trees were felled to make way for more condo towers, I felt my own memories becoming weightless, floating over the newly erected concrete structures like restless ghosts.

My father didn't like what he was beginning to see from our windows as time passed, and I'm sure he wouldn't have liked what I observe now from our balcony, where I sit and read on sunny days. Near the Pineridge complex he loathed, another condominium tower is rising, a construction crane beaming its light into our glen in the evenings, refusing to disappear into the night. Further down the hill, another new condo building dominates the skyline, its beige paint gradually taking on the color of grime.

The three-story wooden house perched on the banks of a creek at the far edge of our glen, which we fondly called "the Tree House" because of the way it seemingly hovered above the vines blanketing the water beneath it, was demolished to make way for another condominium tower that now sits on what has become a dead creek. Nothing remains of the rickety little shack where my father bought ice cream for us on special occasions, or whenever he felt like it. The yellow clapboard house where my fifth-grade classmate's family once lived has been leveled to build another condominium tower; construction paused only briefly after a small prefab office collapsed during a rainstorm into a hole they'd dug for the new building's foundations, killing a young engineer and HR manager who were trapped inside. The building that rose on the spot where they were buried alive now towers over my former elementary school, and the family that lived in the charming clapboard house across the street have since vacated their home for fear of another landslide. Not even a horrific tragedy could put an end to the building frenzy that has besieged our neighborhood, and so why do I still pray for its end, as though I hadn't learned my lesson about the pointlessness of prayer in fourth grade? I was hoping to find a greater sense of permanence in my hometown after losing my father, not realizing how powerless we all are in this relentless push to make way for the new.

* * *

As the city grew, and our neighbors began building on the empty sections of their lots, the trees surrounding our own home remained standing, attracting birds to our yard as our city's forest cover thinned. Growing up, I often saw common sparrows in our yard, an invasive species brought here by Spanish colonizers; it was my father who first pointed out to me the more exotic-seeming gold-breasted bird with bold black streaks over its eyes, its claws gripping a branch of our dying guava tree. When the tree was felled and a young guava sapling was planted in its place, my father spotted what appeared to be the same bird perched atop a stick that had been pushed into the ground to protect the young growth. In the poem he composed about the curious sighting, he wrote:

> The bird, a veteran of flights,
> Back after a long time,
> Perhaps from way across
> The West Philippine Sea,
> Knows it is a mere pole,
> And sits on its tip, silently, head bent,
> Watching the apparition of a tree,
> Waiting for it to grow.
>
> By what infinite patience,
> Faith, or desperation
> This vigil is sustained
> Is really beyond my ken.
> I get the feeling, though,
> That I have merely returned
> To some ancient scene,
> And that I am fated to be part of it—
> That it would not be complete
> Without me.
>
> But does the bird know
> It is no longer the same tree?
> Does it realize it takes
> More than a bird's lifetime
> For a tree to grow?
> *Is it even the same bird?*

Birds identical to the winged visitor my father observed so long ago have since proliferated in our yard, and if he had lived longer, I would've shared with him what I've learned from a birder friend: these beautiful birds are, indeed, from mainland Asia, flying south to warmer climes during the northern hemisphere winter. Along with fantailed and mohawked birds called yellow-vented bulbul that have flocked to our garden in recent years, these gold-breasted birds, called brown shrikes, flit through our guava trees and nibble on fruit, exchanging birdcalls as they swoop across our yard. I wonder if their increased presence in our garden, years after my father wrote his poem, is explained by our thinning forest cover, leaving the birds with only our trees to perch their tired bodies on after their long journey across the sea.

> All the same,
> We look quite like a picture,
> Bird, tree, and I—
> Bird and I equal in vigil,
> In the ache to protect
> Not just this seeming wraith,
> This curious resurgence,
> But also what it evokes:
> The ineffable presence of the former tree.

Perhaps it is the ghost of my father's presence that draws me out onto to our balcony where, just like him, I continue to marvel at the tenacity of this tree and of the birds that find shelter in it. I feel the same longing my father once felt in my own bones as I watch the birds, perhaps descendants of the bird my father once saw, swoop into the tree that grew from the sapling my father once observed so closely. Like a phantom limb, my father lives within me and beyond me; I am his surviving limb, allowing him to transcend his time on earth with my own. Will we all be offered the chance to repeat this cycle of death and rebirth, even as the idea of progress threatens, with every tree felled to make way for a building without history, without any desire to be possessed by what came before it?

* * *

My mother has often told me about another American-style house from her childhood that sat on a hill beyond the yellow bungalow where my fifth-grade classmate used to live. Set far back from the street, it had an ornate birdbath surrounded by a round bench in the middle of its front lawn. She remembers the birdbath quite vividly, since it never failed to enchant her as she walked to her elementary school in the mornings, but she struggles to describe the garden and the house slightly hidden behind the garden's bushes. She remembers the house's pitched roof and gabled windows but not much else, and no trace of it remains in the ordinarily ugly student dormitory that stands in its place and has taken up every square inch of the lot. Her descriptions take on the faded colors of a dream as I try to picture what she once saw; nothing about it feels tangible as I attempt to reach into a past to which she alone has access.

When I listen to her stories of houses and parks long gone, I feel my own connections to Baguio wavering, threatening to snap. As I walk past the condominium towers that have taken the place of a sunflower grove near my house, and a construction site that has obliterated a 1950s-style restaurant where an adult Elizabeth and I met for the first time since we parted ways in third grade, I feel my feet grow unsteady, as though anticipating an earthquake. But gravity keeps my feet planted on the ground, and as I continue running errands that take me down Baguio's narrowing, garbage-strewn streets, I find myself trapped in a city that has become increasingly unbearable, now failing to awaken in me the affectionate loyalty I once held for it.

During the pandemic we limit trips outside of our home, and there are days in which I forget the everyday inconveniences of living in a congested, overdeveloped city. But when I think of what remains of the Baguio my mother knew before I was born, such as the wood-frame cottages of Teacher's Camp and the towering eucalyptus trees along Leonard Wood Road and South Drive, a sudden frenzy to visit seizes me, as though merely thinking of each beloved place from afar might hasten its demise.

I invite my mother to take a walk down the streets of the old Baguio, where trees and colonial homes remain standing, and she says yes, why not—like me, she has developed cabin fever from months spent indoors. We walk up a staircase that takes us to the top of a hill, passing a Frank Lloyd Wright–inspired house with tilted, floor-to-ceiling windows. Plastic bags containing faded electric bills dangle from the property's chain-link fence, and my mother and I wonder aloud if the home is still inhabited, or if its owners failed to come home from overseas this year. There used to be another house, further up the hill, with wide French windows and a large flower garden; I remember passing it on my way home from my first school and seeing through the open windows a group of children gathered around a picture book and an old couple sitting near them. It fell to ruin not too long after I stopped attending the school, and when I left for college, the owners of a Chinese restaurant bought the lot and demolished the house to build a small parking garage for their newest location.

My mother and I are somewhat thankful to be wearing masks, for it makes the climb up these pee-smelling steps a bit more bearable, though we lower our masks to catch our breath as soon as we reach the topmost step. We cross a street lined with shuttered bars and restaurants before being assailed, yet again, by the sharp odor of urine on the other side of the road. We round the bend, walking past a Tudor-style house owned by the Paulinian order of nuns, my mother asking aloud if the nuns have relocated to a quieter location, farther away from the noise of the nearby bars. The Spanish colonial revival home next door has been converted into a café that blares pop music as unmasked customers talk above the din. "How does anyone live here?" my mother yells to me as we watch an old sedan pull into the driveway of the next home. "This used to be a quiet street."

We visit the Pink Sisters Convent where I gave my first confession the year we returned to the Philippines, and we light candles at its outdoor altar before leaving; my mother predicts that, in a few more years, the sisters will also move to a quieter location. We pass more houses with pitched roofs and trees planted in their yards, and she describes how she and her friends would go Christmas caroling on this street as children, collecting so much more from its wealthy inhabitants than from their poorer neighbors in the glen. "Many of those families must be gone now," my mother says, contemplating the empty-looking houses that stare mutely at us like knickknacks on a dusty shelf.

We pass the Pineridge complex, its uniformed guard turning his head to watch us as we approach the white and green house that used to be my first elementary school. After that school moved out due to rising rents, a Korean school moved in, building a gym on what had once been an open field where tall, intimidating students from our school's high school department played volleyball under the hot sun. The gym stands empty now, and so does the house, its floor to ceiling windows inviting us to gaze into its empty living room. As a young girl, I had imagined ghosts from the American colonial era walking up and down the grand staircase, sitting around the fireplace, and luxuriating in the bathtub of the second-floor restroom. The condominium tower we see from our own house rises, unfinished, beyond the ridge on which the house sits, and I feel the panic rising in my chest as I stare through the silence at my former school and the empty yard surrounding it. Should I find relief in what appears to be its quiet defiance as it sits among these other developments surrounding it?

A woman emerges from the wood-frame house behind it to empty out a can of water onto the gravel path. "It doesn't look like the owners intend to sell," I say to my mother, to reassure myself.

"You never know," my mother answers.

We turn around and make our way back to the other end of the street, turning onto Leonard Wood Road. Many of the houses that once stood along this tree-lined strip are gone, and I struggle to remember what they looked like as I glance at the restaurants and shopping malls that have slowly but surely replaced them. I have eaten at some of those restaurants, and have bought imported goods from the luxury supermarket housed inside the shiny new building that was carved into a hill nearby, so why should I complain about the changes this street and city have undergone? And yet I do not feel the same quiet pull the old houses once exerted on me; I instead find myself growing numb as I walk past the concrete structures now standing in their place.

We learn that the old farmhouse atop a hill, seemingly kept safe for many years from greedy developers by its high iron fence and a grove of pine trees, has been bulldozed. Two forlorn-looking trees tower over a clearing on which a billboard, advertising the name of a developer and a drawing of a high-rise, now stands. My mother is crestfallen. "They sold too," she says sadly, and we stare at the clearing in silence before deciding to move on.

We take a left into Teacher's Camp and are assailed by the stench of raw sewage flowing through its waterways as we descend the cracked steps, past white and green cottages the Americans built to house the academics they shipped across the Pacific to establish our educational system. From what I know, the Americans also built the waterways of this teachers' retreat in the mountains, but I never had to cover my nose as a child, when I visited the camp on school trips to watch athletic games and attend exhibits. My mother thinks the untreated sewage flows down from the encampment of tin shacks sitting on a hill overlooking the camp, but I wonder if the impoverished hilltop inhabitants are solely to blame for the overpowering smell that seeps through our masks. Baguio has grown bigger, and developers have poured cement into our creeks while funneling the shit of too many condo residents into an overburdened sewerage system. Our leaders appear unworried by this, continuing to welcome developers to build on what little is left of what the city once was.

My mother guides me up the dilapidated steps of a grassy hill, where a bust of Dr. José Rizal, our national hero, presides over the gardens and century-old wooden structures beneath him. She tells me that when she and my father were younger, they often climbed these steps to sit beneath Rizal's bust, and when we reach the topmost step, food wrappers and soda bottles litter the platform on which we stand. At the age of thirty-five, Rizal was executed by firing squad for writing two novels, *Noli me tangere* and *El filibusterismo*, that inspired an armed revolution against Spanish colonial rule, leading to our sale by Spain to the United States in 1898 and the beginning of the Philippine-American War. Our new colonizers eventually defeated us, and though Rizal predicted this in his essay, "Filipinas dentro de cien años" or "The Philippines a Century Hence," it wasn't something he'd hoped for; his wish was for Spain to either extend to us the same rights enjoyed by its citizens or to grant us independence. He objected to colonialism but held ambivalent feelings for our colonizers, recognizing how the ideals of Enlightenment, with which he came in contact while studying in Europe, gave clarity and purpose to the anticolonial struggle by upholding the basic, irrefutable humanity of the colonized. He fought for the basic freedoms of his countrymen while being eagerly shaped by the intellectual traditions of Europe, and I wonder what he would have felt when the Americans posthumously made him the national hero of their new colony, hoping to teach us the concepts of Western democracy through his example. Would he be filled with admiration as he watched the American academics train Filipino teachers in their conference halls to be beacons of democracy, or would his idealism be tempered by a wry skepticism of the colonizer's benevolent intentions?

My gaze sweeps over the terraced gardens flanking the steps to Benitez Hall, whose polished wood floors and light-filled French windows once left me with a quiet, unexplainable longing as a girl. The Americans built this teachers' retreat on what had been ceremonial land for the Indigenous Ibaloi; perhaps I am being naive in wanting to hold on to the relics of our colonial past, a past that itself erased what came before from our collective memory? The far-reaching educational system the colonial government implemented remade us in their image, and though it made education more accessible, I wonder if it also awakened in us a lust for the invisible promises of the future, which we attempt to reach for again and again by obliterating our past. Perhaps I simply do not possess the same desire for progress that so many in this city seem to have, but I also struggle to find my footing in this place I call my hometown when it can no longer hold the shape of my own memories.

* * *

As my eyes flit from my book to our blossoming guava tree, and then down to our flowering bougainvillea bush, I imagine bulldozers coming for our house, excavating the earth where these trees stand, digging up the bones of our beloved pets buried by my father in our yard. He dug the grave of our favorite dog, Joker, particularly deep to honor her human qualities; I can imagine construction workers casting her bones aside, digging ever deeper into the earth. The urge to stay put seizes me, if only to watch over the graves of my childhood pets and the trees that are nourished by the soil in which they're buried.

At dinnertime, my mother and I observe the unlit windows in our neighbors' homes—like our own two-story home, most of the houses aren't fully inhabited, their owners deceased or dying, their children living in Manila or overseas. My mother has seen too many of the homes of her childhood friends torn down in recent years. She is quite sure that our house, and the half-vacant homes surrounding it, are being monitored by developers for signs of a potential sale. Her siblings in California won't be returning to claim the house as theirs—since their lives are no longer here, their interest in the property amounts to cents rather than sentiment. I prefer not to think of the day they'll cut down our trees and bulldoze my childhood home, but my mother tells me it will happen, whether or not I decide to stay.

I try to enjoy what is left of the garden that my grandparents cultivated and my parents cared for. This land is my own Eden, allowing me rest as I continue to nurse my grief. Am I not looking toward the future as I sit among the trees, finding echoes of what I witnessed the previous spring in a tree that sheds its leaves before releasing its blossoms, and in returning birds that look just like the birds I've seen in previous years? I don't know when all of this natural beauty will disappear, but perhaps I can claim the future my father once saw for himself as he watched a strange bird perching beside his guava sapling. I am his echo, communing with the echoes of everything he once saw:

> But it is instinctive to return—
> Perhaps to commune, and with kindred spirits,
> Revive impossible nostalgia,
> All as though we were rehearsing
> For infinity—or waiting, at least,
> For some time outside of time,
> For some metaphor to confirm us.
>
> Doubtless, these coincidences,
> These serendipities,
> All start from yearning,
> And travel across oceans
> Like even the merest bird.

ACKNOWLEDGMENTS

It was in Cristina Garcia's first year seminar at the Michener Center for Writers that I began writing nonfiction in earnest. While my classmates crafted poems, stories, and visual narratives as a response to the books we read about war, dictatorship, and colonialism, I found myself reflecting on my own memories of growing up in the Philippines and America, and facing the task of contending with my homeland's complicated history as I pieced together memories on the page. In doing so, I saw how the stories I carried in my body, through accidents of history, were worth telling. I am grateful to Cristina Garcia and my cohort at the Michener Center for creating a safe space for me to achieve this vulnerability in my writing.

Although I've mainly seen myself as a fiction writer due to my academic training, nonfiction served as my refuge while I grieved my father's death, giving me a vehicle for processing my sorrow at a time when I doubted my own capacity for continuing on as a writer. I have my mother, Priscilla Supnet-Macansantos, to thank for welcoming me back to Baguio, where I rested, recuperated, and wrote my way through my grief and into the light. This book wouldn't have been possible without my father, Francis C. Macansantos, who cultivated in me a love for the written word that carried me forth in the midst of my grief. Writing—his first love—is what keeps us connected across the distances.

I am indebted to the editors of the following journals, magazines, and presses where essays in this collection first appeared: *Colorado Review*, the *Hopkins Review*, *Bennington Review*, *Lunch Ticket*, *About*

Place Journal, the *Pantograph Punch*, *SBS Australia*, *Another Chicago Magazine*, *TAYO Literary Magazine*, *Vol. 1 Brooklyn*, *Katherine Mansfield Studies*, *New Naratif*, and Telling Our Stories Press. Your faith in my work keeps me going. Special thanks to Melissa Sipin and the editorial staff at *TAYO* for their hard work in helping shape "Becoming a Writer: The Silences We Write Against." Our collaboration was a pivotal moment in my growth as an essayist, teaching me the art of telling a compelling story while speaking my truth. I am also grateful to Robert Atwan of the *Best American Essays* series for awarding Notable citations to four essays in this collection, providing necessary encouragement in my journey as a nonfiction writer and memoirist.

This book's existence in the world would not have been possible without the inimitable Marisa Siegel, whose faith in this scrappy manuscript steered it toward publication. I'd like to thank her, the Press Board, and the team at Northwestern University Press for their belief in this project, for their tireless work in making my words shine, and for all their efforts in producing a beautiful book. I am deeply grateful for the life-changing opportunity to share these stories about the people I've met, the life I've lived, and my amazing papa with readers.

I'd like to thank the Michener Center for Writers at the University of Texas at Austin and the International Institute of Modern Letters at the Victoria University of Wellington for nurturing and supporting my work and giving me the freedom to hone my voice on my own terms. James A. Michener, your generosity of spirit opened so many doors for this Filipino writer who yearned to see the world. Elizabeth McCracken, Michael Adams, Jim Magnuson, Oscar Cásares, Allan Gurganus, Brigit Pegeen Kelly, Anthony Giardina, Elizabeth Butler Cullingford, Damien Wilkins, thank you for lighting my path with your wisdom and kindness. Debbie Dewees and Marla Akin, thank you for making Austin, Texas, my second home. Clare Moleta, thank you for doing the same for me in Wellington, New Zealand, and Katie Hardwick-Smith, thank you for helping me through some difficult times in Wellington.

Much gratitude to the artists' residency programs that generously provided me with the time, space, and support to grow and flourish as a writer: the Kimmel Harding Nelson Center for the Arts,

Hedgebrook, Storyknife Writers Retreat, the I-Park Foundation, Monson Arts, and the Black Mountain Institute.

Much gratitude to friends and comrades near and far, old and new, who read my work, offered feedback, or simply cheered me on: Greg Marshall, Whitney Cox, Andrew Viloria, Dennis Gupa, Grace Talusan, Katrina Lallana, Melissa Santos, Maria Nela Florendo, Nancy Florendo, Heather Aruffo, Susanne Pari, Carlos O. Aureus, Jose Dalisay, Gerald T. Burns, Jose Wendell Capili, Ellen Darion, Nick Carbó, Amor Tan Singco, Niccolo Vitug, Charles Viloria, Christine Yra-Garcia, Joy Ebuen-Yra, Nelson Turgo, Antonio Ruiz-Camacho, Donna Miscolta, Chanel Clarke, Chad Nichols, David B. Smith, Brendan Daniel Sheridan, Peter Cox, Lydia Blaisdell, Catherine Robertson, Bekky Thorne, Erica Watson, Mary Miller, Romylyn Boñaga, Penelope Endozo, Razilee Ramos, Sheila Navarro, Jean Munson, Cherry Lou Sy, Chloe Bernardo, Stephanie G'Schwind, Colette LaBouff, Alejandro Heredia, Charlotte Wyatt, Joshua Cohen, Kim Treviño-Kiraly, Kellen Braddock, Niko Galindez Manipol, Rachel de Vera, Jose Reyes, Jocy Ru, Andrew Zubiri, Patty Enrado, Vickie Costina, and Elizabeth Calinawagan.

Thank you to the Macansantos, Supnet, and Puno clans for inspiring me with your stories and supporting me throughout this journey.